Word for Windows 6.0
Slick Tricks

· · · · · · · · · · · · · · · ·

Kay Yarborough Nelson

RANDOM HOUSE
ELECTRONIC PUBLISHING

New York

Word for Windows 6.0 Slick Tricks

Produced and composed by Parker-Fields Typesetters Ltd.

Published in the United States by Random House, Inc., New York, and simultaneously in Canada by Random House of Canada, Limited.

Manufactured in the United States of America

First Edition

0   9   8   7   6   5   4   3   2   1

ISBN 0-679-79175-2

Trademarks

New York   Toronto   London   Sydney   Auckland

Word for Windows 6.0 Slick Tricks

Contents

• •

Acknowledgments

Many thanks to all who made this book possible: Tracy Smith, Senior Editor at Random House and Michael Aquilante, Project Editor. These truly professional editors got the job done right, and on time, and it is a pleasure working with them.

Introduction

This *Slick Tricks* series is based on a simple idea: You don't have to know a lot about a program to get some real power from it! All of the software you buy today is incredibly rich in features, though most of us will use only a few of them because we don't want to wade through the manual or spend hours working through exercises.

But beyond the programs' intimidating interfaces lies a wealth of tricks that you can master easily—without taking a complex tutorial on a program's whole feature set, or thumbing through a huge doorstop-sized tome. You can flip through the pages of this *Slick Tricks* book, find a topic that's related to what you're working on, and see how to do a trick or use a shortcut that will make your work a lot easier.

Why Slick Tricks?

Most of these tricks are just that: tricks, short statements about how to use a keyboard shortcut to do something faster, or how to go through a back door to get a complicated sequence done quickly. We're not starting from ground zero and teaching you the program's basics, though. To get the most from a *Slick Tricks* book, you'll at least need to be familiar with the program's absolute basics, such as selecting with a mouse (if you're in a Windows or Macintosh book) or reading a prompt (if you're in a DOS book).

Using a *Slick Tricks* Book

You can think of a *Slick Tricks* book as a cookbook—browse its pages and try out a "recipe" or two. But these are fairly "right-brained" books, so you may need to browse until you find the recipe you need.

These books offer basic tricks—the ones you'll use all the time—and include tricks for customizing, printing, managing your documents, and any special features of the programs. These short, friendly books can't possibly cover *all* the features of a program or system, but neither would you want them to.

Trick

Tip

Trap

Sidebar

You'll see different icons in a *Slick Tricks* book. The professor indicates a hands-on procedure or trick, showing you how to do something. A "Tip" gives you a helpful, general hint about how to approach a task or work out a solution to your problem. "Traps" tell you procedures to avoid, and "sidebars" provide background material for a particular topic. These *Slick Tricks* books won't always take you step by step through every possibility and every detail, but programs today have incredibly good Help systems, and you can use them to get details about a specific topic. So, do that.

Each *Slick Tricks* book follows the general conventions of the program or system it's about. You'll find the keys you need to press in boldface type and what you actually need to type in sans-serif type, like this: Press **F12** and type weekly report. In all of these, if you need to press two keys at once, you'll see them with a plus sign between them, like this: Press **Ctrl+Z**.

You're on Your Way

· ·

That's it! You can figure out the rest as you go along. For example, if you see any instructions that talk about screen color, just ignore them if you have a monochrome monitor. You may see tips and tricks repeated in different chapters, but that's to keep you from jumping back and forth in the book. Have fun with these books and amaze your friends with what you can do!

Word for Windows 6.0
Slick Tricks

Chapter 1

· ·

Basic Slick Tricks

ALTHOUGH THE TRICKS IN THIS CHAPTER are simple, don't be fooled: Simple tricks—the ones you use for things you do every day—are the real timesavers and keys to productivity. After all, a few keystrokes multiplied over hundreds of times are a lot of keystrokes. These slick tricks add up to saved time that you can spend thinking about other work or even being away from the computer.

Menu Tricks

· ·

Usually, using a menu is the slowest way of issuing a command in Word. But as there are going to be times when using menus will be unavoidable, here are a few tricks for using them.

Using Keyboard Shortcuts to Open Menus

Just press the **Alt** key, release it, and then type the underlined letter in the menu's name to open it. For example, typing **Alt** and **a** opens the Table menu. Once the menu is open, type the underlined letter of the command you want to use. For example, **Alt**, **a**, **i** chooses Insert Table from the Table menu. (This is how you'll see them in this book, with each key separated by a comma.)

Once you've opened one menu, you can use the right and left arrow keys to open the other menus.

Use Windows' Standard Shortcuts

There are a few shortcuts that are almost universal in all Windows programs, and Word is no exception. You may find these easier to remember than the program's own shortcuts:

Ctrl+C Copy

Ctrl+X Cut

Ctrl+V Paste

Ctrl+Z Undo

Function Key Shortcuts

Word also has a set of function key shortcuts. These are harder to remember and the vast majority of them aren't listed on the menus, but if you use a command frequently, you may find a few of them worth memorizing. For example, **Go To** is **F5** and **Save As** is **F12**. **Find Again** is **Shift+F4** (not listed on the menu) and **Repeat Typing** is **F4**. I'll mention a few of these whenever they seem useful, but don't try to memorize them all or you'll go crazy.

No F11 and F12 Keys?

If you don't have the function keys F11 and F12 on your keyboard, use **Alt+F1** and **Alt+F2** instead. They work most of the time in shortcut combinations.

Window Tricks

There are all sorts of slick tricks hidden in a typical Word window. In this section, you'll see a lot of them.

Mousing Around

Although there's lots of emphasis in this book on keyboard shortcuts, Word is also full of hidden mouse tricks. And sometimes it's really more convenient to use the mouse than the keyboard. Figure 1.1 shows a typical window and the locations where you can click or drag with the mouse.

♦ Click on a menu's name to open the menu.

♦ Click on a button to carry out its function.

♦ Click on a window's Minimize icon to hide it, its Maximize icon (not shown) to make it full-screen size, or its Restore icon to make it the size it was before.

♦ Click on the scroll arrows to move up and down, one line at a time.

♦ Click on a downward-pointing arrow to display a drop-down list.

♦ Click on the tab indicator and then on the ruler to set a tab.

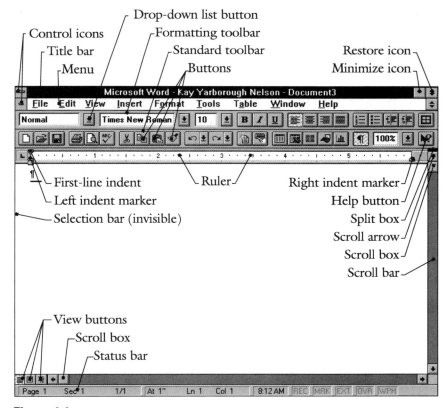

Figure 1.1 **Features of a basic Word screen**

- ◆ Drag a window by its title bar to move it (if the window is less than full-screen size).

- ◆ Drag the scroll box to a different location in the scroll bar to go to that area of a document.

- ◆ Drag the split bar to split a window into two panes.

- ◆ Drag a window's border inward to make the window smaller, or outward to make it bigger.

- ◆ Drag the left and first-line indent markers on the ruler to set indents.

- ◆ Drag a toolbar to reposition it.

- ◆ Drag a tab marker to move a tab stop. Drag it completely off the ruler to delete a tab stop.

- ◆ Double-click on a Control icon to close the document (the lower Control icon) or to exit from Word (the upper Control icon).

- ◆ Double-click on a window's title bar to maximize it or restore it to the size it was previously.

- ◆ Double-click on a toolbar to display it as a small floating toolbar (Figure 1.2) or return it to its original size.

- ◆ Double-click on the Split box to split the window in two or return it to one view if you've already split it.

- ◆ Double-click on the ruler to open the Page Setup dialog box.

- ◆ Double-click on a tab marker to open the Tab dialog box.

- ◆ Double-click on the status bar to open the Go To dialog box.

Displaying Toolbars

Click with the right mouse button on a toolbar to display the Toolbar shortcut menu (Figure 1.3). To display another toolbar, select its name by clicking with the left mouse button.

To hide a toolbar that's being displayed, select its name to uncheck it (it will have a check mark next to it).

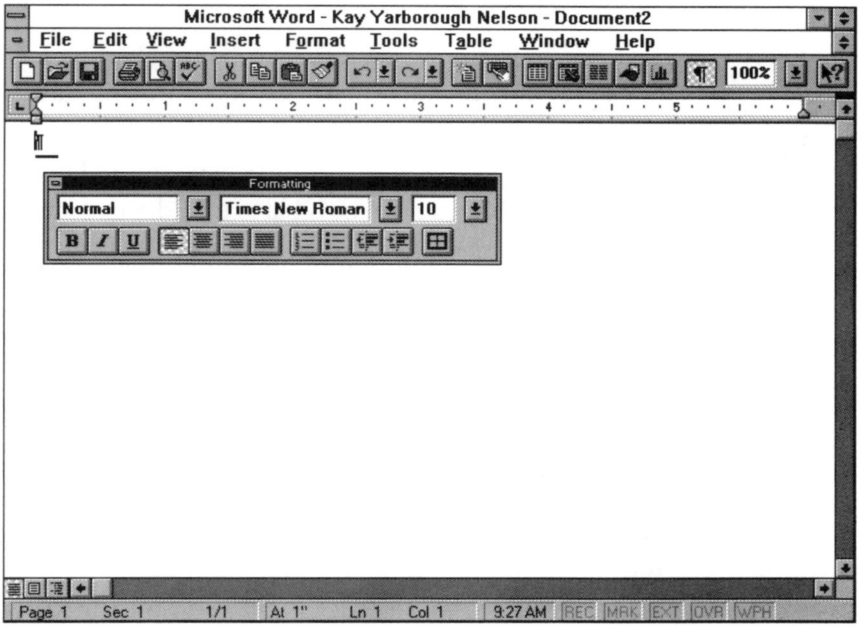

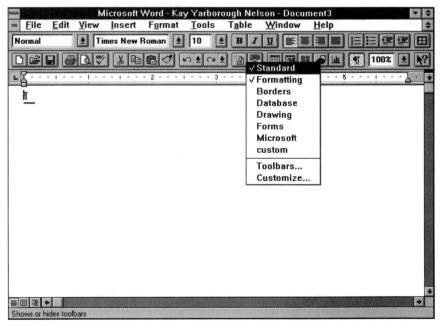

Figure 1.2 A floating toolbar

Figure 1.3 The Toolbar shortcut menu

Splitting a Window

You can split a window into two panes (Figure 1.4) by choosing Split from the Window menu (**Alt, w, p**) or by dragging the split bar located above the scroll arrow in the vertical scroll bar. Double-click on that split bar to split the window into two panes. This is a great help if you need to be able to view two parts of a document at the same time—to check a cross reference, for example.

Working with Two Views of a Document

You can also look at two different views of the same document if you split it. Say that you want to see the structure of your document by looking at it in outline view, but you want to edit its text in normal view. Just split the window and choose a different view for each pane (see Figure 1.5).

Information at a Glance

Don't overlook the useful information on the status bar. It shows the page number, section number, total number of pages in the document, and the time.

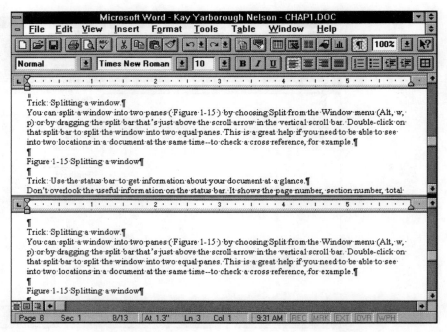

Figure 1.4 Splitting a window

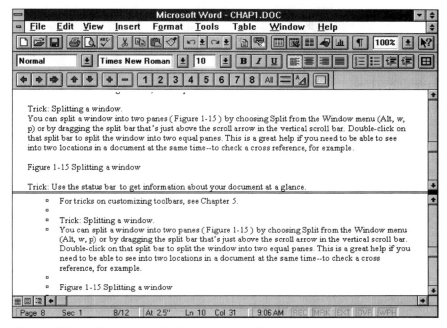

Figure 1.5 **Splitting a window into outline and normal views**

Double-click on the status bar to get the Go To dialog box and you can then move quickly to another part of your document.

The Arrange All Command

Use the **Arrange All** command in the **Window** menu to look into all your open documents (**Alt**, **w**, **a**). This will instantly give you a peek into all the documents you have open.

Moving between Open Documents

To display an open document, choose it from the Window menu, which lists all the documents you have open. To switch to a different document quickly, choose its name from this list.

Opening Documents Quickly

The File menu lists the last nine documents you have opened. You can open any of these documents by choosing its name from the list on the File menu (Figure 1.6). The Window menu displays only the documents that are currently open.

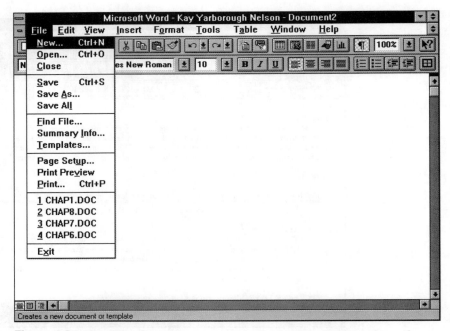

Figure 1.6 The last documents you worked with are listed on the File menu.

Switching between Programs

If you're running Word as well as some other programs in Windows, use this trick to switch among them:

1 Press **Ctrl+Esc** to bring up the Task List.

2 Use the arrow keys to highlight the program you want.

3 Press **Enter** to switch to it.

Or press **Alt+Tab** repeatedly and stop when you see the program you want to switch to.

Hidden Tricks for the Control Menu

All Windows programs have Control icons (Figure 1.7) that drop down menus when you click on them. The program's Control menu lets you move windows and size them, among other things. Actually, it's pretty useless except for its keyboard shortcut **Alt+F4**, which lets you exit Word without double-clicking on the Control icon. It's much easier to move and size windows by using the mouse. The document's Control menu also lets you move from document to document.

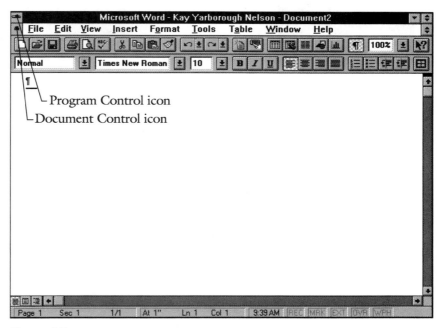

Figure 1.7 The Control icons

Instead of clicking on these Control icons, you can open the menus with shortcuts:

Alt+Spacebar opens Word's Control menu.

Alt+Hyphen opens the current document's Control menu.

Neat Tricks with the Document Control Menu

You can use the shortcuts listed on the document Control menu to move from one document to another and to close the window you're working in:

Ctrl+W closes the window you're in. If the document has been modified but not saved, Word asks if you want to save it. **Ctrl+F4** does the same thing if you are used to that shortcut.

Ctrl+F6 moves you to the next document you have open. This is a great time saver if you've opened a lot of documents.

Ctrl+F10 maximizes a window that's less than full-screen size.

Five Views for Displaying Documents

You can display your documents in five different views, each one good for certain tasks:

♦ Use Normal view (**Alt**, **v**, **n**) for typing the bulk of your text and for most character formatting.

♦ Use Outline view (**Alt**, **v**, **o**) to set up an outline, or to see the structure of your document if you've set up headings as outline entries.

♦ Use Print Preview in the File menu (**Alt**, **f**, **v**) to see how your document will look when it's printed—complete with line numbers and lines between columns (which won't show up anywhere else), headers, footers, page numbers, and so on. Print Preview also lets you see a double-page spread. And, unlike earlier versions of Word, in Word 6 you can edit in Print Preview.

♦ Use Page Layout view (**Alt**, **v**, **p**) for editing text columns, headers, and footers, or inserting graphics.

♦ Use Master Document view (**Alt**, **v**, **m**) for working on a long document with different chapters or sections.

In addition, you can zoom in on part of a document to get a close-up view, or get a clean screen that is uncluttered with toolbars and rulers (see the next trick).

Figure 1.8 shows which buttons will switch you to the various views.

Getting a Clean Screen Quickly

Sometimes you'll want to get all of the toolbars and rulers out of your way. There's a slick and quick way to do this: Choose **Full Screen** from the **View** menu (**Alt**, **v**, **u**). Then, to return to the regular editing window, just click on the **Full Screen** button that appears.

Use Zoom for Quick Magnification

The Zoom box on the Standard toolbar (the one with a number and a percent sign in it) lets you magnify or reduce the view of the section of the document you're looking at. If you're editing a document that's formatted for legal-sized (8.5 by 14-inch) paper or one that's to be printed in Landscape orientation (sideways), you may want to change

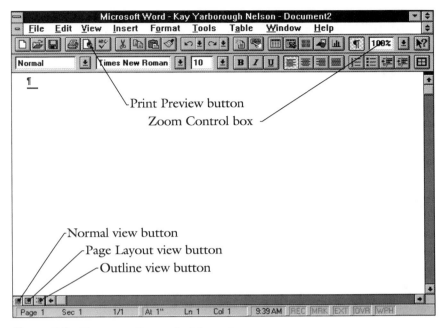

Print Preview button

Zoom Control box

Normal view button

Page Layout view button

Outline view button

Figure 1.8 **Buttons for switching views**

from the default magnification so that you can see the whole page, or to zoom in and get a close-up view.

Click on the arrow next to the Zoom box to pick a percentage from the drop-down menu, or type a percentage into the box itself. Choosing Page Width will reduce the document to fit within the right and left margins if it's been enlarged so that it's too big to fit on the screen.

There's also a Zoom command on the View menu. Using the Zoom box or the Zoom command (**Alt, v, z**), you can choose:

Page Width to reduce or enlarge the document to fit within the right and left margins.

Whole Page to fit the page on the screen. This is good for viewing documents that are in Landscape (sideways) orientation.

Two Pages to see two pages at once (available in the Zoom box only).

Many Pages to see two or more pages at once (available from the Zoom command only). Click on the tiny monitor and drag to choose the number of pages you want to see.

Notice that you can't use the last three choices unless you're in Page Layout view or Print Preview.

Quickly Displaying the Page Setup Dialog Box

You can double-click on a ruler to open the Page Setup dialog box. From there, you can adjust margins, change paper size, and so on.

Turn Off Background Repagination

To speed up Word, turn off background repagination if you know you'll be working in Normal view for a while. That way, Word won't have to repaginate as you're editing the document and you should see an increase in speed.

To turn off background repagination, choose **Options** from the **Tools** menu (**Alt, t, o**), click the **General** tab, and uncheck the Background Repagination box. This doesn't work if you are in Page Layout view.

Moving Page by Page in Page Layout View

See those double-arrow icons at the bottom of the vertical scroll bar in Page Layout view (Figure 1.9)? Click on them or use the PgUp and PgDn keys to move through your document page by page.

A Very Useful Trick: Return to a Previous Location Instantly

Shift+F5 returns you to the place in your document where you last made a change. If you want to go back to the last three places in your document where you've been working, keep pressing **Shift+F5**. This is a very useful trick to use after you've been editing footnotes, headers, or footers, or moving from one page to another. You can also use Shift+F5 to return to the place you were working on when you last exited from the document.

Dialog Box Tricks

Use the speed select shortcut instead of scrolling through lists. Just type the first letter of an item's name to go straight to that part of the list.

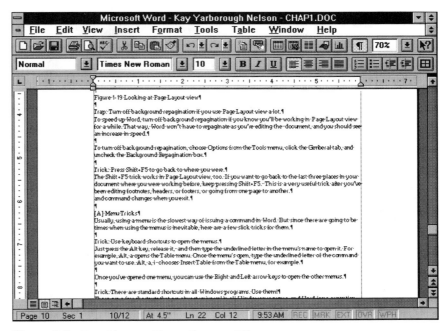

Figure 1.9 **Looking at Page Layout View**

It's much faster than scrolling. Type that key again to get to the next item that starts with that letter if the first one isn't the one you want.

If a list is closed, all you see is a downward-pointing arrowhead, indicating that it's a drop-down list. Click on it or press a key when it's highlighted to open it. Figure 1.10 shows the list that drops down from the List Files of Type menu.

Type Your Way through Dialog Boxes

If you're a touch typist, taking your hands off the keyboard to reach for the mouse can really slow you down. However, it's possible to type your way through dialog boxes without using the mouse once. You won't often run across all of these items in any one dialog box, but these tricks will let you keep working at the keyboard:

- ◆ Press **Tab** to move clockwise among options. Press **Shift+Tab** to move you counterclockwise.

- ◆ Press **Enter** to choose the OK button.

- ◆ Press **Ctrl+Tab** to move between sets of options.

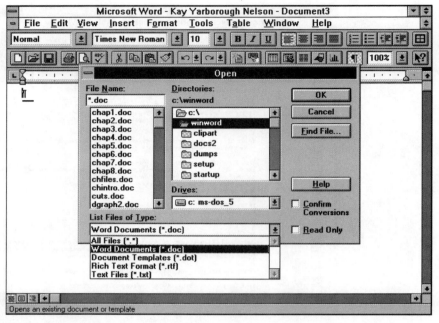

Figure 1.10 Opening a drop-down list

♦ Press the **Spacebar** to check a box.

♦ Press **Alt** and type the underlined letter of a command to select it.

♦ Type the first letter of an item in a list to highlight it.

♦ Press any key when a pop-up or drop-down list is highlighted to open it.

♦ Press **Esc** to close the dialog box (a *very* handy trick in itself).

Selecting Several Items

Some dialog boxes let you select more than one item in a list. To pick more than one, press Ctrl and click on the items you want.

Help!

• •

The Help system in Word works like Help in other Windows programs, but as usual, there are a couple of slick tricks you can use with it.

Press F1 for Help

Pressing **F1** brings up the Help system without having to choose from the menus. It's much faster.

The Help Search Button

If you know what you're looking for, it's much, much faster to enter the topic you need help on in the Search box and let Help find it for you than it is to scroll through the alphabetical list. If you know even one word that's part of the topic you need help on, use the Search feature.

Use the Index in Help

Choose **Index** from the **Help** menu (**Alt, h, i**) and click the button of the letter you want. This is fast, but not as fast as searching for the exact topic you want.

Use the Back and History Buttons

Lots of folks ignore these useful buttons, but they can quickly back you out of a dead-end search. Back (or **Alt+b**) takes you to the last topic you got help on, and History (**Alt+t**) lets you go back to any topic you've looked at before and start a new branch down a different trail.

Context-Sensitive Help

If you need help understanding what a particular keystroke combination, menu command, or icon does, you don't need to open a Help window or use the Index or Search features.

When you press **Shift+F1** or click the Help button on the toolbar, the pointer changes to a question mark. Now press a key combination, click on an icon, or select a menu command, and Help for that subject automatically opens. This can be a great aid in deciphering some of the stranger icons on the Toolbar.

Keeping Help Always on Top

If you're looking at a How To Help window (a procedure window), you'll often want to keep the step-by-step instructions visible as you try out the procedure. To do this, click on the **On Top** button in the **How To** box, or choose **Always on Top** from the **Help** menu off the main **Help** menu.

Open Documents from Help

If you're looking at a Help window, you can choose **Open** from its **File** menu to open a help file. You can also print help topics from Help's File menu if you want to keep a hard copy of the instructions for carrying out some procedure.

Keeping Help Windows Out of Your Way

Sometimes you'll want to get a Help window out of your way while you work, but keep it handy so you can refer to it quickly. To send the Help window behind the document window, just click anywhere in your document window. To bring the Help window back, press **Alt+Tab** until you see it again.

Tricks for Opening and Saving Documents

You'll spend a lot of time opening and saving documents in Word, so here are some slick tricks to help you along the way.

Keyboard Shortcuts

Instead of using the File menu to open and save documents, get accustomed to these keyboard shortcuts:

Ctrl+O (or **Ctrl+F12** if that's what you're already used to from using previous versions of Word) brings up the Open dialog box.

Ctrl+S (or **Shift+F12**) saves the document you're working on, assuming you've already saved it at least once. If you haven't saved it before, you'll get the Save As dialog box the first time you use this shortcut.

F12 brings up the Save As dialog box so you can save a document under a different name.

You can also use the Standard toolbar for opening a new document, opening saved documents, and saving documents. The first three buttons on the left (if you haven't changed your toolbar) let you do this (see Figure 1.11). But it's much easier to save as you work by simply pressing **Ctrl+S** every so often.

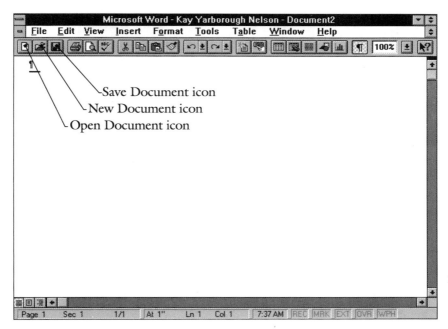

Figure 1.11 The buttons for New Document, Open Document, and Save Document

You Can Open Several Documents at Once

When you're looking at the Open dialog box, just press **Ctrl** and click on the names of the documents you want to open all at once. Press **Shift** and click to select a range of documents whose names are right next to each other.

Protecting a Document from Being Changed

If you want to work on a document you don't want to change, click on **Read Only** when you open it.

In the bottom-right corner of the Open dialog box is a tiny Read Only box (see Figure 1.12). Check it if you want to be able to read the document you're opening, yet protect it from inadvertent changes. You'll be able to change it, but when you go to save it, you won't be allowed to save it unless you use the Save As command and save the changed version under a different name.

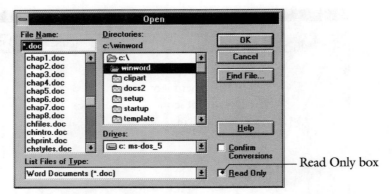

— Read Only box

Figure 1.12   The Read Only box in the Open dialog box

Changing the Default Directory

Word normally shows you the contents of the C:\WINWORD directory when you use the Open or Save As commands. To have it automatically show you a different directory:

1 Choose **Options** from the **Tools** menu.

2 Choose the **File Locations** tab.

3 Select **Documents** and click the **Modify** button.

4 In the **Modify Location** dialog box (Figure 1.13), set the directory you want to use for storing documents.

The next time you go to save or open a document, you'll see the contents of that directory in the Open or Save As dialog boxes.

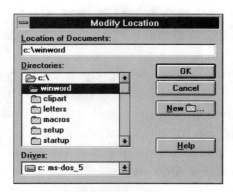

Figure 1.13   Changing the default directory

Showing All the Files in a Directory

If there aren't any Word files in the directory you have opened, no files will be listed under File Names. Go down to the drop-down list under **List Files of Type** and choose **All Files (*.*)** to see all the files that are in that directory.

Switching to Another Drive

Sometimes you'll be working with files on floppy disks instead of on your hard disk. To tell Word to use drive A or B (or any other drive), press **Tab** to move to the Drives box and type the letter of the drive. You can also click in the Drives box and select a drive from the drop-down list, but you may find that the keyboard shortcut is faster.

Backup Copies or Fast Saves?

You can't have both backup copies and fast saves. Fast saves take much less time than full saves, since Word saves the complete revised document when it does a full save, but saves only the changes you've made when it does a fast save. However, backup copies that the program makes automatically (see the sidebar "Safe Saves" later in the chapter) require full saves. That is why the Allow Fast Saves box in the Options dialog box is unchecked when you check Always Create Backup Copy.

Saving and Exiting: The Fast Goodbye

If you're exiting from Word, just double-click on the program's Control icon in the upper left corner of the screen or press **Alt+F4**. You'll be prompted to save each document that you haven't saved before you exit.

You can also use this trick to exit from Windows. Just double-click on the Program Manager's Control icon or press **Alt+F4** when you're in the Program Manager. Windows will take you back to each program that's running, and you'll be prompted to save any unsaved documents. It is faster to let Windows do this than to switch to each program to save your documents.

Safe Saves

The automatic saves and backup copies that Word makes aren't really backups; they're just duplicates of your work. It's a great idea to use these features, but if your hard disk crashes and you haven't made copies on a separate disk, you've still lost your work. Real backups are stored on a different medium—such as a floppy disk or a tape. For belt-and-suspenders protection, store these copies away from your usual work area—in case of fire or your typical local disaster (earthquakes, where I live).

To set backups in Word, choose **Options** from the **Tools** menu (**Alt**, **t**, **o**). Then type s for Save or click on the Save tab. You'll see the screen in Figure 1.14.

You can also get to the Save options dialog box by clicking the **Options** button in the **Save As** dialog box. This may be easier to remember than using the Options command on the Tools menu.

Choose **Always Create Backup Copy** if you want Word to save the previous version of a document (with a .BAK extension instead of a .DOC extension) each time you save it. For example, if you save MAY.DOC with this feature checked, a backup copy of the old version of MAY.DOC, named MAY.BAK, will be made automatically. Each time you save MAY.DOC, MAY.BAK is changed to reflect the previous version. If your work calls for getting a previous version of a document back—after a round of reviews, for example—turn this feature on by checking its box.

Click on **Allow Fast Saves** if you want Word to save only the part of the document that you've changed since the last time you saved it, This is faster than a normal save, because Word lists the changes you've made instead of redoing the whole file. Normally this feature is on, but there are circumstances when it's best to turn it off. When you're ready to compile an index or transfer a Word document to another program, it's a good idea to turn off Allow Fast Saves and do a regular save so that the file is in exactly the right condition.

You can't have both Always Create Backup Copy and Allow Fast Saves on. If you want the entire backup version made, you must save completely every time you save a document.

The last, most important Save option is **Automatic Save Every:**. Check this box and enter a number in the minutes box so that Word will automatically save your document at the desired intervals. If the power shuts off, the next time you start Word the documents you were working on are displayed automatically with (Recovered) in their titles, and you can get your work back. The only work you will have lost will be whatever you did after the last automatic save. How many minutes should you set? It depends on how much work you're willing to lose. I have mine set to 5 minutes—but I live in an area where the power goes out frequently.

Lights Getting Dim? Use Save All.

Word has a slick Save All command that will save all the documents you have open. Choose **Save All** from the **File** menu (**Alt, f, l**) to use it. It's much faster than going to each document and saving them one by one.

Closing All Open Documents

Word also has a handy Close All shortcut, but you need a trick to use it: Press **Shift** and hold it down as you open the **File** menu and you'll see that Close has changed to Close All.

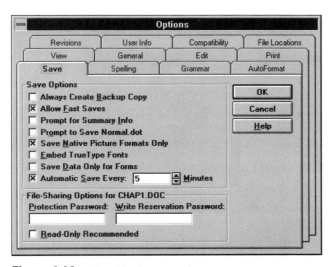

Figure 1.14 Word's Save options

Opening a New Document

The shortcut **Ctrl+N** opens a blank editing window, ready for you to start a new document.

Opening a New Document and Using a Template

Instead of using the **Ctrl+N** shortcut, choose **New** from the **File** menu. You'll get a dialog box (Figure 1.15) where you can choose a template or a Wizard.

A template is a document that's already set up, ready for you to use. Often, all you'll have to do is fill out a dialog box or two to create the document. A Wizard is different: It takes you step by step through the process of creating a document so that you can learn how to do it. Chapter 8 has more tricks for using templates and Wizards.

Using Find File

Word has a wonderful Find File command built into the Open dialog box. With this handy command, you can find a document if you can remember part of its name. Click on the **Find File** button, and you'll see the dialog box in Figure 1.16. If you've used Find File before, you'll see the last search you set up.

The simplest kind of search you can make is for file names. In the **File Name** box, enter the name of the file you're looking for. Use wildcards to represent the characters you're not sure about in the document's name. (See the sidebar "Using Wildcards.") For example, entering

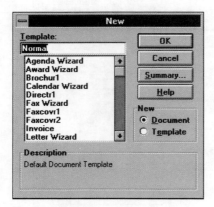

Figure 1.15 Choosing a template or a Wizard

Using Wildcards   Just as in poker, wildcards are special characters that can stand for other characters, like wildcards stand for other cards.

   The asterisk represents any number of letters (or none at all), and the question mark (?) represents any one character (or none at all). So, *.* stands for "everything" (any or all of the eight characters in a file name plus any three-character extension) and ?LTTR.DOC stands for any files that begin with one character and are followed by LTTR.DOC, such as 1LTTR.DOC, ALTTR.DOC, and so on. You can use wildcards to speed up operations on files that have similar name patterns so that you can manipulate several files at a time.

*.doc tells Word to look for all files starting with any combination of characters and ending with the .doc extension. Entering ???.doc tells Word to search only for files with three characters in their names and ending with a .doc extension.

   To search your whole hard disk, make sure the Location box reads **c:** and check the **Include Subdirectories** box.

Deleting Files within Word

You don't have to use the File Manager or DOS to delete a file; you can do it within Word, as long as the document isn't open. Use the Find File command and look for the document you want to delete. When Word

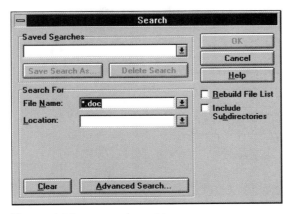

Figure 1.16   Finding a file

finds it, highlight its name. Click on the Commands button and choose Delete from the list.

Fancy Searching

The Find File command is actually very sophisticated. If you've used summary information in your documents (see the next trick), you can do all kinds of fancy searching with this information. Click on the **Advanced Search** button and then on the **Summary** tab, and you'll see the dialog box in Figure 1.17.

Say that you remember that the document you're looking for has the words *Martha* and *Washington* in it. In the **Containing Text** field, enter Martha & Washington. Or, you can put a space between them if you like.

But what if you're sure it has *Martha* but you're not sure about *Washington*? To look for documents that have *either* word in them, enter Martha,Washington. Be sure to separate them with a comma. You can also put a space between them if you like.

And if you know you're looking for the name *Martha Washington*, type "Martha Washington" in quotes. That tells Word to look for that exact phrase, not two separate words.

This trick works only for Word documents that have summaries. But the preceding trick lets you locate any file, no matter which program created it.

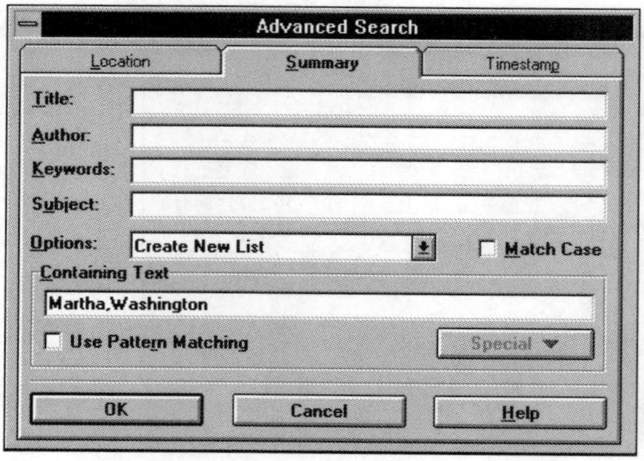

Figure 1.17   **Searching through summaries**

Using Summaries

Word keeps track of a lot of information about your document, such as the title, subject, any comments or key words you want to add, the date the document was created and last saved, the length of time spent working on it, how many words and characters it contains, and so on. Word keeps track of much of this information automatically, whether you've created a summary or not.

To add summary information, such as subject, key words, and comments, to the document you're working on, choose **Summary Info** from the **File** menu (**Alt, f, i**).

To add summary information to a document you've already created, select the document in the **Find File** dialog box, click the **Command** button, and choose **Summary**. You'll see the screen in Figure 1.18.

If you want to be prompted for information for a document summary each time you save a document for the first time, choose **Options** from the **Tools** menu (**Alt, t, o**), type **s** for Save, and then check the **Prompt for Summary** dialog box.

If you don't want to be prompted for this information, just uncheck Prompt for Summary. You won't have to deal with this particular dialog box each time you save a new file unless you turn the option back on by checking it again.

Get Statistics about a Document

Do you want to get a word count or see how long you've spent on a particular report? Choose **Summary Info** from the **File** menu (**Alt, f, i**)

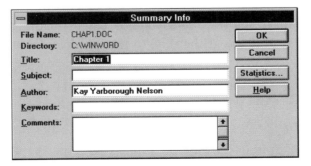

Figure 1.18 Viewing document summary information

Document Statistics		
File Name:	CHAP1.DOC	Close
Directory:	C:\WINWORD	Help
Template:	C:\...\TEMPLATE\NORMAL.DOT	
Title:	Chapter 1	
Created:	10/28/92 12:47 PM	
Last Saved:	12/01/92 9:06 AM	
Last Saved By:	Kay Yarborough Nelson	
File Size:	74,240 Bytes	
Revision Number:	26	
Total Editing Time:	112 Minutes	
Last Printed:		
Statistics:		

Pages	13
Words	6,517
Characters	29,375
Paragraphs	280
Lines	644

Figure 1.19   Checking document statistics

and click on **Statistics**. You don't have to have created a summary to get this kind of information (Figure 1.19).

To see the summary information about a document you're not working on, choose **Find File** from the **File** menu. In the **Listed Files** box, select the document you want information about. Then choose **Summary** in the **View** box. If you haven't made a search before, Find File will bring up a Search dialog box.

Save Documents before Checking Summaries

The Document Statistics information is based on the document as it was when you last saved it. If you want to check a word count in the document you're working on, for example, save it before you check the summary statistics. That data is based on the condition of the document as it was at the time of the last save. Be warned.

Slick Ways to Start Word

• •

Tired of double-clicking on Word's icon in the Program Manager? There are all kinds of different ways to start Word, and most of them let you do a slick trick at the same time.

Starting Up with a Blank Screen

Use this trick to start Word without having to stare at a blank new document until you can figure out which document you want to work with today. Exit Word, go to the Windows Program Manager, and select the Word icon (the icon for the program, not the one for the group). Press **Alt+Enter** and you'll see the Properties dialog box (Figure 1.20). Add **/N** to the end of the command line box and click OK. Now when you start Word, you'll no longer automatically get a blank document.

Starting Up with the Last Open Document

If you like to start Word with whatever document you last had open, change the Properties dialog box by typing **/Mfile1** at the end of the command line. From now on, Word reopens the last document you had open before you exited.

Starting with a Specified Document

You can start Word with as many as nine documents. The trick is to start it "manually"—either from the DOS prompt, the Windows Program Manager, or File Manager's Run box, instead of double-clicking on its icon. Use this command:

winword *document name*

where *document name* is the name of the document or documents you want to open, in the order you want them opened. If they aren't in Word's directory, give the path to where they are. For example:

winword c:\winword\docs\doc1.doc

c:\word2\docs\reports\doc2.doc

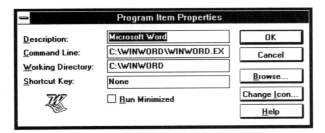

Figure 1.20 You can edit Word's startup command line.

opens the documents DOC1.DOC and DOC2.DOC, which are stored in two different directories.

Starting Windows and Word Automatically

If you want Word to start every time you turn on your computer, you can edit your AUTOEXEC.BAT file. Assuming that you're in the Windows Program Manager, double-click on the Notepad icon; then choose **Open** from the Notepad's **File** menu. Type c:\autoexec.bat in the box and press **Enter**.

Press **Ctrl+End** to go to the last line in the file; then type win winword. Choose **Save** from the **File** menu and then double-click on the Notepad's **Control** icon to close it. From now on, when you turn on your computer, Windows will start and Word will launch.

Starting Word When Windows Starts

If you drag the Word icon into the StartUp group in the Program Manager, Word opens automatically each time Windows starts up. It's easier than editing your AUTOEXEC.BAT, as in the previous trick. This way, Word starts only when Windows starts, but it doesn't set up Windows to start automatically each time you turn on your computer.

Open the StartUp group and the Microsoft Word group. Highlight the Word icon; then press **Ctrl** and drag it to the StartUp group window. Now Word will launch when Windows starts.

Starting Word with Its Default Settings

To start Word without using any templates or options you've set, choose **Run** from the Program Manager's **File** menu and then enter this command in the Run box:

    winword /a

Starting with a Macro

To start Word with a macro, follow the *winword* command above, with a slash (/), an m, and then the macro name (with no space between the m and the macro's name):

    winword /mmacroname

You can specify as many macro names as you like. For example, the first macro might create your letterhead, the second one set up a specific format, and the third one type boilerplate text. Chapter 8 has more about macros.

What Next?

· ·

With these basic slick tricks in mind, it's time to look at other tricks you can use for those time-consuming chores: typing and editing.

Chapter 2

• •

Editing Tricks

YOU CAN'T GET AWAY FROM TYPING and editing what you've typed. Fortunately, with a few of the slick tricks in this chapter, you can make both tasks faster and more enjoyable.

Typing Tricks

• •

What do you do most in a word processing program? Typing, right? So use the slick tricks in this section to streamline your typing chores.

Quick Retyping

Here's a simple and perhaps obvious trick that can save you a great deal of time over the long run. Don't bother to delete selected text and then type new text. Just select the text to be deleted and start typing. Your new text replaces the text that was selected. This trick also works in the dialog boxes that appear with text selected and ready for you to use, such as the Save As dialog box where the document's current name is highlighted when it opens.

Typing Replaces Selected Text

If you've come to Word for Windows from Word for DOS or from another DOS word processing program, you may not appreciate the built-in feature that lets you replace selected text by typing over it, because you'll undoubtedly forget the first few times and lose some text. If you mistakenly replace selected text, use the **Undo** command to get the original text back. To turn off this feature so that this will never happen to you again, use the handy **Options** command on the **Tools** menu (**Alt, t, o**). Click on the **Edit** tab, or type **e** for Edit, and uncheck the **Typing Replaces Selection** box (see Figure 2.1).

Word will now work like Word for DOS: New text that you type appears to the left of selected text.

The Typing Replaces Selection feature can really drive you nuts when you're searching, because when Word finds what you searched for, it selects it. If you press a key, that selected text disappears and you're left looking at the character whose key you pressed.

Instant Retyping

You won't have to retype text you've just typed as long as you remember this slick trick: Press **Ctrl+Y** or choose **Repeat Typing** from the **Edit** menu. Pressing **F4** also repeats typing.

Word stores everything you type in a buffer, which isn't flushed until you use another command. You can type and format text, move to a new location and press **F4**, and what you just typed is inserted there. Word also stores the correction keystrokes you made, such as pressing **Del** or **Backspace**.

This trick is a great timesaver, even if you're not duplicating text. Just use repeat typing for paragraphs that are very similar to the paragraph you want, and then edit the text that appears in the new location.

Changing Capitalization

Word makes it really easy to change capitalization. Select the text whose capitalization you want to change and then keep pressing **Shift+F3** until it's the way you want it. Try it and see.

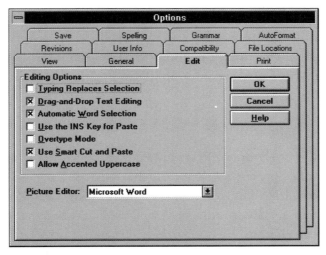

Figure 2.1 Typing Replaces Selection is checked by default, but you can turn it off.

You can also choose **Change Case** from the **Format** menu but the keyboard shortcut is faster.

Use these handy shortcuts to switch to all caps or small caps:

Ctrl+**Shift**+**A**   ALL CAPS

Ctrl+**Shift**+**K**   SMALL CAPS

Using Special Mode Keys

Some keys and key combinations in Word can toggle you quickly between one mode and another. For example, pressing the Ins key toggles between Insert mode, which inserts text between characters, and Overtype, which replaces what's been typed with what you're typ   ;
now. Overtype is good for editing data in columns that have equal-sized entries because you can just type over what's already there without selecting it first.

Other toggle keys:

Num Lock   Lets you type numbers from the numeric keypad

Caps Lock   Lets you type in capital letters

Toggling Keyboard Shortcuts

Some keyboard shortcuts are toggles. Use them once to turn functions on, twice to turn functions off. For example, if you press **Ctrl+B**, highlighted text becomes boldface. Pressing **Ctrl+B** again removes the boldface.

Using Undo

Word very thoughtfully includes an Undo feature that undoes an action. To undo, press **Ctrl+Z** or **Alt+backspace**. To undo something before the very last thing you did, keep on pressing **Ctrl+Z** or **Alt+backspace**.

There's a Redo button as well as an Undo button on the Standard toolbar (Figure 2.2). Click on the curved arrow to undo or redo an action. Click on the downward arrow to see a list of things that can be undone or redone. If you undo something, you can usually redo it by clicking on the **Redo** button. Think of Redo as undoing Undo. By the way, you can Undo the last *one hundred* things you did.

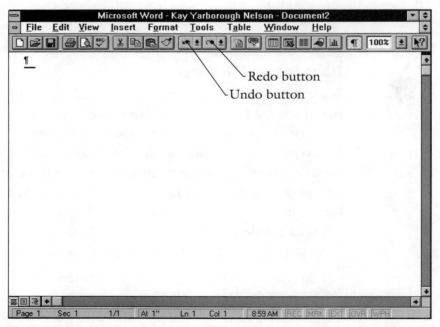

Figure 2.2   The Redo and Undo buttons

Don't Undo or Redo Too Many Things at Once

Be careful! It's really easy to redo the last four or five actions you've undone and get hopelessly lost as to what you have or haven't done, especially if you've just done a search-and-replace operation. Using Undo and Redo are a little risky if you try to redo or undo several things at once. Undoing one thing at a time is safest.

Tricks for Selecting Text

Selecting text is something you do all the time in any word processing program. Word has a lot of built-in shortcuts and secrets for selecting not only text, but also tables, charts, graphics, and other objects.

Selecting Text with the Keyboard

You can select text with the mouse, the keyboard, or a combination of the two. Usually, selecting with the keyboard is much faster because you don't have to move your hands to reach for the mouse. And there are a *lot* of keyboard selecting tricks.

Selecting with F8

Use the **F8** key to select text. To select a word the insertion point is in, just press **F8** twice. To select the entire sentence, press **F8** three times. For the whole paragraph, press **F8** four times. To select the entire document, press **F8** five times (or press **Ctrl** and **5** on the numeric keypad).

If you're selecting text and the beginning of the selection starts on your screen but the end is somewhere beyond the screen's boundaries, F8 is a neat way to select it instead of Shift-clicking to select, because you don't have to keep the Shift key held down while you locate the end of your section.

Pressing **Shift+F8** reverses the process: If a paragraph is selected, pressing **Shift+F8** selects the current sentence. Pressing it again selects the current word.

Speed Selecting

Use this little trick to extend highlighting to the next occurrence of a character without taking your hands off the keyboard. Press **F8**; then type the character. For example, to select to the end of a sentence ending in a period, press **F8** and type a **period**. Press **F8** and press **Enter** to select to the next paragraph mark.

Press **Esc** if you change your mind about what you were going to do with that selection. Otherwise, anywhere you click with the mouse will extend the selection. So will typing any key. The selection doesn't disappear when you press Esc; click elsewhere on the screen to turn off the selection. You can also double-click on the **EXT** indicator on the status bar to turn off the way F8 extends selections.

The Keyboard Selecting Secret

If you know the keyboard shortcut for moving from one place to another in a document, you can use that same shortcut to select text. Just press Shift along with that key combination.

For example, **Ctrl+Home** moves you to the beginning of a document, and **Shift+Ctrl+Home** selects to the beginning of the document. **Ctrl+End** moves to the end of a document, and **Shift+Ctrl+End** selects to the end.

Press **Ctrl+A** to select the entire document. Think of it as "All."

Selecting Letter by Letter

If you select text by dragging over it using the mouse, Word selects the text word by word. You can turn this feature off if you want to select letter by letter, but it's usually better to just use the keyboard. Just press **Shift** and a **Right** or **Left arrow** key. Pressing **Shift** and an **Up** or **Down arrow** key selects line by line.

Selecting with the Mouse

OK, you *can* select text with the mouse, and sometimes it's really faster than using the keyboard, especially if you're going back after typing a document to tune up its formatting. Selecting graphics is almost always faster with a mouse. Here are a few quick ways to select with a mouse.

Selecting by Clicking the Mouse

Double-click on a word to select it. To select more than one word, put the cursor in the invisible selection bar on the far left of the screen; it will change to an open arrowhead. Click once to select a line. Double-click to select the whole paragraph.

Selecting by Dragging the Mouse

You can also select text by dragging the mouse over it. Place the cursor at the beginning of the selection you want to make; then press and hold the left mouse button and move to where you want the selection to end. Release the mouse button, and the highlighted text will stay highlighted. You can also drag in the invisible selection bar.

Shift-Clicking with the Mouse

Shift-clicking is another way to select with the mouse. Place the cursor at the beginning of the text to be selected, press the **Shift** key, and then click at the point where you want the selection to end. Everything in between will be selected.

Selecting Just About Anything with the Mouse

Here's a hidden secret: Ctrl-click in a sentence to select just the sentence. To expand your selection sentence by sentence, drag the mouse to the next sentence. You'll keep selecting by sentence until you release the Ctrl key.

Here's another hidden secret: Select something, keep the mouse button down, and drag, just as in the preceding tip. You'll select another of what you just selected. Say you selected a word; you'll select word by word as you drag the mouse. It works on paragraphs, too. The trick is not to let go of the mouse button. If you do, you'll move the text when you drag the mouse.

Another hidden secret: Ctrl-click in the selection bar in the left margin to select your entire document. It will all be selected, even the parts you can't see. (Remember, there's also the Ctrl+A keyboard trick, which is usually faster.)

Deselecting the Document

To turn off the highlighting and deselect the document, press the **Right arrow** key to go to the end of the document, or press the **Up arrow** key to go to the beginning of the document.

Selecting One Character at a Time

Often you'll want to select just one character, but Word selects word by word. To select letter by letter with the mouse, choose **Options** from the **Tools** menu; then click on the **Edit** tab and uncheck the **Automatic Word Selection** box. It is easier, though, to press **Shift** and an arrow key to select letter by letter.

Using the Keyboard and Mouse Together

Sometimes it's easier to use a combination of the keyboard and the mouse to select text. Click at the beginning of the selection you want to make; then press the **Shift** key and click at the end. All the text in between will be selected.

Selections from Hell

Sometimes you'll change your mind about what you want selected, but you can't turn off the selection highlighting. Every time you move the insertion point, you just select more text. Pressing **Esc** won't work, either. Here's the secret: Press **Esc** and then press a cursor key (one of the arrow keys will do nicely).

Inserting the Date and Time

Don't bother typing the current date or the current time. Just press **Alt+Shift+D** to insert the date or **Alt+Shift+T** for the time.

To automatically update a date or time that has been inserted this way, select it and press **F9**.

Resetting the Date and Time

Are the date or time, or both, not correct? Reset your computer by using the **Date/Time** icon in **Windows' Control Panel**. You'll have to do this twice a year for Daylight Savings Time unless you live in one of those delightful parts of the country that ignores Daylight Savings Time.

Tricks for Copying, Moving, and Cutting

Word lets you move and copy text as well as graphics or items you've inserted from other programs. Use these slick tricks to speed up the process.

Moving Text Quickly

This is a very slick trick. First, select the text or graphics that you want to move. Then press **Ctrl** and click with the right mouse button where you want the moved text to appear. You may find this method is easier to get used to than dragging and dropping.

Drag Selected Text to Move It

Dragging and dropping text to move it is often much faster than cutting text and then pasting it in its new location. Double-click on a word to select it; then, holding the left mouse button down, drag it to the place where you want it and release the mouse button. When you can drag and drop, the cursor changes to an arrowhead with a tiny box, and the

Dragging and Dropping

Dragging and dropping is a quick way to copy or move text and graphics. Select the item you want to move; then put the cursor anywhere in the selection, press the left mouse button, and drag the selection to where you want it. When you have it where you want it, release the mouse button.

You can also drag and drop text and graphics that you've selected *between windows*. To move a selection, just drag it to another open window and release the mouse button.

Until you get used to dragging and dropping (it takes a little practice), you may wind up with text in places that aren't quite where you wanted it. To undo a drag-and-drop operation and put the text back where it came from, don't try to drag it back: Just press **Ctrl+Z** for Undo.

insertion point becomes a moving dotted line showing where the text will appear if you click in that location.

If you don't see this special cursor, dragging just extends your selected text.

Dragging a sentence or paragraph is easier. Click three times in the paragraph to select it. Then drag it to the new location and release the mouse button.

Copying Text by Dragging and Dropping

If you're copying text, you'll find that Word's drag-and-drop technique is indispensable—once you get used to it, that is. Just select the text you want to copy, press **Ctrl**, and drag the insertion point to the place where you want the copy to appear. Let go of the mouse button, and Word inserts a duplicate of the text you selected.

Drag-and-Drop from One Window to Another

Many folks don't know this, but you can drag text or a graphic from one window and drop it into another window. The trick is to get the windows arranged so that you can see into each one—the one you're dragging from, and the one you're dropping into. To do this, choose **Arrange All** from the **Window** menu.

An Even Easier Copy Shortcut: Ctrl+C

Use the universal Windows shortcut **Ctrl+C** to copy selected text. I say "text," but you can copy anything you can select—graphics, equations, and so on.

Whatever you copy using Ctrl+C goes to the Windows Clipboard, where you can paste it into other Word documents or into other Windows programs. To see what's on the Clipboard, double-click the Clipboard Viewer icon in the Windows Main group. The Clipboard can hold only one item at a time. The next time you copy or cut something, it replaces what was on the Clipboard. But when you copy or move text by dragging and dropping, the Clipboard remains unchanged.

Ctrl+**Ins** is another shortcut for Copy that's not listed on the menus. It's a relic from earlier versions of Windows, before the (almost) universal shortcuts Ctrl+C, Ctrl+X, and Ctrl+V were adopted.

And if they're not enough different ways to copy, there's yet another one: Click on the **Copy** icon on the **Standard** toolbar once you've made your selection; then move the cursor to the new location and click on the **Paste** icon.

Copying with Shift+F2

There's also a keyboard shortcut you can use to copy selected text. I hardly ever use it, but it does have one subtle feature: When you copy text by pressing **Shift+F2** (instead of using either Ctrl+C, choosing Copy from the Edit menu, clicking on the Copy icon, or using Ctrl+Ins—Word gives you *lots* of ways to copy), the selection doesn't replace what's on the Clipboard. So if you have one selection in the Clipboard, you can copy another one with **Shift+F2** and paste them both in different locations. This is a neat way for pasting two separate things, such as two addresses, in several documents or locations.

You can also do a "copy from" if you're already at the location where you want the moved text to appear. Just press **Shift+F2** and when you're asked "Copy from where?" select the text you want to move, then press **Enter**.

Watch the status bar for these "Copy to where?" and "Copy from where?" messages or you may get confused by the Shift+F2 shortcut.

This trick works only within Word; don't use it to copy items to other Windows programs.

Moving with F2

You can move text or items by first cutting and then pasting them into a new location. Word also has a subtle key combination that lets you move text without using the Clipboard and replacing what's there. Just select the text or item you want to move and then press **F2**. You'll see "Move to where?" on the status bar. Click where you want to move the text to and press **Enter**.

You can also do a "move from" if you're already at the location where you want the moved text to appear. Just press **F2**; when you're asked "Move from where?" select the text you want to move and then press **Enter**.

This trick also works only within Word; you can't use it to move text to another Windows application.

Keyboard Tricks for Moving Paragraphs

Word even has hidden slick tricks for moving paragraphs using the keyboard. If you're heavily into keyboard shortcuts, try this. You have to see it to believe it, because it's a little awkward to explain.

With the insertion point in the paragraph you want to move, press **Alt+Shift+Up arrow** to move it *before* the paragraph right above it. Press **Alt+Shift+Down arrow** to move it down past the next paragraph. If you've added blank lines between paragraphs, you'll have to press the key combo twice.

You can quickly transpose one paragraph with another this way, or you can keep on pressing Alt+Shift+Up or Down arrow to move the paragraph to wherever you want it.

Cutting and Pasting Text

To cut text to the Clipboard, select it and then press **Ctrl+X**. You can also use the rather obscure shortcut **Shift+Del** or click on the **Cut** icon on the **Standard** toolbar (the Scissors).

Once you have cut or copied something to the Clipboard, you can paste it as many times as you like (until you copy or cut something else to the Clipboard, of course).

Ctrl+**V** is the easy shortcut for Paste. You can also use **Shift+Insert**, or paste by clicking on the **Paste** icon on the **Standard** Toolbar (the one that has a tiny clipboard on it).

If you'd like to be able to use Ins to paste, instead of going into Overtype mode when you press the Ins key (which is really only useful in tables or columns where you're correcting entries that are equal in length), choose **Options** from the **Tools** menu and then click on the **Edit** tab or type **e** for Edit. Then check the **Use the INS Key for Paste** box.

Deleting Entire Words

Delete entire words with **Ctrl+Del** and **Ctrl+Backspace**. If you hold down the **Ctrl** key while pressing the **Delete** key, you'll delete the whole word to the right of the insertion point, as long as the insertion point is between words. (If it's within a word, you'll delete to the end or beginning of the word.)

Press **Ctrl+Backspace** to delete the entire word to the left of the insertion point when it's between words. Keep **Ctrl** down and press **Backspace** repeatedly to delete words, one at a time, to the left of the insertion point.

Tricks with AutoCorrect and AutoText

Word for Windows added new AutoCorrect and AutoText features that make typing almost painless. With AutoText, you can store selections of text and graphics that you will use more than once, or use in several different documents. Use AutoText for storing large selections, such as a graphic or a table, or several paragraphs of boilerplate text. Use Auto-Correct for proper names, phrases of a few words, hard-to-spell items, and words you habitually mistype. You can use it for storing graphics, too, but in general it's best to use AutoCorrect for items you use frequently and AutoText for items you use only from time to time. With AutoCorrect, the stored item appears as you type; with AutoText, you first decide when and where you want the item to be inserted, then type its name and click on the **AutoText** button on the **Standard** toolbar (Figure 2.3).

Using AutoText

To use AutoText to store a selection of text or a graphic that you will use again, select the item, then click on the **AutoText** button on the **Standard** toolbar. You can accept the name Word suggests, or type another name for the selection (as many as 32 characters, and you can also include spaces). Then click on **Add**, and your selection will be added to the list of AutoText entries (see Figure 2.4).

Store the AutoText entry in your Normal template if you want it to be available in all your documents.

To use your AutoText entry quickly, without reaching for the mouse, just type its name in your document and press **F3**. Pressing **Alt+Ctrl+V** works, too, but it's harder to remember.

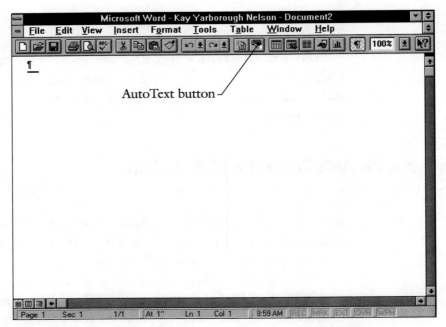

AutoText button

Figure 2.3   The AutoText button on the Standard toolbar

A Quick Tip for AutoText

If you include a blank space at the end of a word or sentence when you create an AutoText entry, the text will appear in your document with the proper space around it, and you won't have to go back and add the space.

Keep the Formatting of an AutoText Selection

Word stores your selection as plain text unless you include the paragraph mark in the selection. When you insert that text in other documents, it will take on the format of the document you insert it in. If you want to keep the formatting of a paragraph, such as a letterhead, be sure to include the paragraph mark. To see these marks, click on the **Show/Hide Paragraph** button on the **Standard** toolbar (it looks like a paragraph mark).

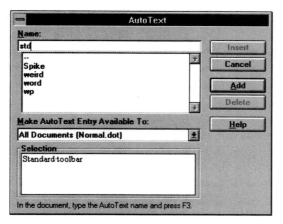

Figure 2.4 Creating an AutoText entry

A Shortcut to the Shortcut

Instead of typing a complete AutoText name, you can type just enough of it to tell Word which entry you want. For example, if you've stored several addresses as 1add, 2add, 3add, and so on, all you have to do is type **1a** and press **F3** to insert the entry. That is, unless you have another entry that begins with 1a.

Forgot Your AutoText Names?

It's easy to set up a lot of AutoText entries and then forget the shorthand you used to name them. If you can't remember the name, choose **AutoText** from the **Edit** menu (**Alt, e, x**) and pick the name you want from the list. Look in the Preview part of the dialog box to see what the item contains.

AutoCorrect Your Typing

This feature is neat! AutoCorrect can correct your bad typing as you type. For example, I'm unable to type the word *document* without typing it as *docuement*. I made an AutoCorrect entry for *docuement*, and Word now corrects it automatically. You'll love this trick.

Just choose **AutoCorrect** from the **Tools** menu (**Alt, t, a**). Then, in the dialog box you'll see (Figure 2.5), type the word as you mistype it

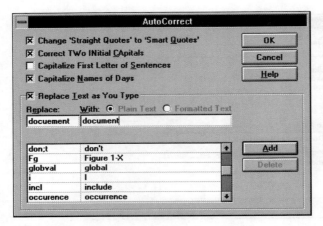

Figure 2.5 Creating an AutoCorrect Entry

in the **Replace** box and type what you want it replaced with in the **With** box. Then click on **Add** and **OK**.

From now on, whenever you type (or mistype) that word followed by a space, Word will automatically correct it by replacing it with whatever you entered in the With box.

Making "Hard" Words Easy

Use AutoCorrect to replace proper names and phrases that are hard to type. If there are "hard" words and phrases that you have to type over and over, use AutoCorrect instead of struggling through typing them. You'll never have to type *hypolipoproteinemia*, or *Michael R. Zamczyk*, or an address and zip code in full again.

Although you can use spaces in AutoText names, you can't use them in AutoCorrect names. Of course, you can use spaces in the entries for either.

Don't Use Real Words As AutoCorrect Entries

Think about it. If you use a word that you type regularly as an Auto-Correct entry, Word substitutes the AutoCorrect entry for it every time you type that word. Use a unique abbreviation, or put a symbol in the entry, such as *%name* or *&address*.

Creating an AutoCorrect Entry from Existing Text

It's often a lot faster to select what you want as the replacement text instead of typing it in the With box. You could copy it and paste it in the With box, but Word figures out what you want to do if you just select the text and then choose **AutoCorrect** from the **Tools** menu. You can select as many as 255 characters for an AutoCorrect entry.

An added benefit of this trick is that the formatting of the text gets saved as well. When you simply type in the With box, you get regular, unformatted text.

Editing AutoText and AutoCorrect Entries

If you decide later that you want to add text or graphics to AutoText and AutoCorrect entries, just make the changes to the text in your document, select it, and choose **AutoCorrect** from the **Tools** menu or click on the **AutoText** button on the **Standard** toolbar. Select the item's name from the list and click on **Add**. Word asks you to confirm that you want to replace the old entry.

Whoops! I Got an Autocorrect Entry I Didn't Want.

Nobody's perfect, and you can't always pick the right unique abbreviation to use for each and every AutoCorrect entry. The day will come when you need to type *1add* or some other odd word, and you get an AutoCorrect entry for that word. Just press **Ctrl+Z** for Undo when that happens.

Turning Off AutoCorrect

This feature drives some folks nuts, so Word gives you an easy way to turn it off. Choose **AutoCorrect** from the **Tools** menu (**Alt, t, a**) and uncheck the **Replace Text as You Type** box.

Spike Your Selections

Word has a special type of AutoText entry that's called the Spike. Put simply, anything you select can be put on the Spike so you can insert it in a different location in your document, just as you'd stack papers on the old-fashioned metal spike that used to be seen in newspaper offices. Unlike items that go to the Clipboard, where each newly cut or copied item replaces what was there before, things that you put on the Spike stay there—it can hold quite a few selections, both text, graphics, and a combination of the two. You can insert selections more than once, and in different documents, which makes this a very handy trick for moving text and graphics around in your documents.

Once you've made a selection, to put it on the Spike, press **Ctrl+F3**. Word automatically creates an AutoText entry named Spike. The item you selected is cut and placed on the Spike, added to what's already there. To paste it into a document, move the insertion point to where you want the item to appear and type **spike**. Then press **F3** or **Alt+Ctrl+V**. If you can't remember either of these keyboard shortcuts, click on the **AutoText** button on the **Standard** toolbar, after you type **spike**. Everything on the Spike is inserted, so just delete the items you don't want.

If you want to paste the contents of the Spike and clear it, just press **Ctrl+Shift+F3**. Exiting from Word also flushes the Spike.

Seeing What's on the Spike

To check what's currently on the Spike, choose **AutoText** from the **Edit** menu and select **Spike** from the list (Figure 2.6). In the Preview box you'll see the contents listed, although you won't be able to see large multiple items.

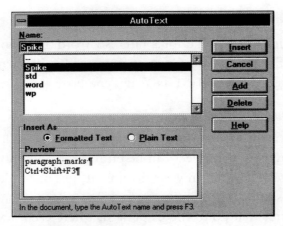

Figure 2.6   **Previewing the contents of the Spike**

Tricks for Navigating through Your Documents

There are keyboard shortcuts for navigating through documents which are much faster than scrolling. Here are a few of the most useful; there are lots more obscure ones:

Ctrl+**Home**	To go to the beginning of a document.
Ctrl+**End**	To go to the end of a document.
Home	To go to the beginning of a line.
End	To go to the end of a line.
Ctrl+**Right arrow**	To move right word by word.
Ctrl+**Left arrow**	To move left word by word.
Ctrl+**Up arrow**	To move to the beginning of the current paragraph.
Ctrl+**Down arrow**	To move to the beginning of the next paragraph.
PgUp	To move up one screen of text at a time.
PgDn	To move down one screen of text at a time.

Drag-and-Drop and Scroll at the Same Time

Once you've selected text or graphics and you're dragging it to drop it somewhere off the screen, just drag it to the edge of the window and the display scrolls in that direction.

Moving the Insertion Point after Scrolling

Normally, the insertion point doesn't move when you scroll by using the mouse, so you can look all around in your document before you decide where you want to start typing next. But if you scroll and then press any of the arrow keys, you'll go back to where you started scrolling from.

Going Back to Where You Were

If you've gone to a far-away place in a long document, you can quickly get back to where you were by pressing **Shift+F5**. This is one of the obscure function key combinations that is actually very worthwhile to memorize.

Here's another hidden secret: Press **Shift+F5** again to go back to the next-to-last place where you were. Word stores the last *three* locations, so you can even use Shift+F5 a third time. The fourth time you press Shift+F5, you'll end up where you started.

Return to the Location of the Insertion Point

Note that when you reopen a document you were working on previously and then press **Shift+F5**, you will return to the location of the insertion point when you saved the document. Remember this one; it's a real timesaver if you work in long documents.

Word Can't Find Your Last Place

You have to do something so Word can find your place again. If all you do is move the insertion point—say you're just reading text, for example—Word can't find the last place you were. If you want to be able to get back to that place with **Shift+F5**, either do something (like selecting a word or letter) or try this slick trick: Press **Backspace** and then **Alt+Backspace**. You won't have done anything to your document, but Word registers your action so that you can return there later.

Hidden Slick Tricks in the Go To Dialog Box

To open the Go To dialog box quickly, double-click on the status bar or press **Ctrl+G**. It looks pretty straightforward (Figure 2.7), but it has some hidden slick tricks.

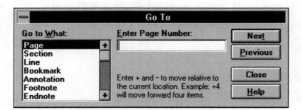

Figure 2.7 Using the Go To dialog box

To go back a number of pages, type a minus sign before the number. For example, to go back two pages, enter p–2, or just –2. Entering +2 takes you forward two pages.

To go forward a certain number of lines, type an l and a plus sign. For example, typing l+20 moves you forward 20 lines.

To move by a certain percentage through your document, type the percent sign. For example, to move roughly to the halfway point of a document, assuming you're at the beginning, type 50%.

Using a Table of Contents to Go to a Specific Page

If your document has a table of contents, you can go to a page simply by double-clicking on that page number in the table of contents.

Scroll Bar Secrets

Drag the scroll box to go roughly to that relative location in a document. Drag to the middle to go to the middle of the document, or to the bottom to go to the end, for example.

Using an Outline to Navigate

Although outlining isn't usually considered a way of navigating through your documents, it can be. The use of an outline enables you to see your document's structure easily. If you have set up your document as an outline (see Chapter 8), it's easy to collapse the outline so you can see just the headings. Once you're looking at the headings, you can quickly see what section you want to go to.

Using Bookmarks to Navigate

Word has a Bookmark feature that's very simple to use. If you work in long documents and find yourself jumping around from place to place, use the Bookmark. Just put the insertion point at the spot you'd like to mark; then press **Ctrl+Shift+F5**. (You can also choose **Bookmark** from the **Edit** menu if you hardly ever use Bookmarks and don't want to remember this key combination.) Type a name for your Bookmark (don't uses spaces, though) and press **Enter**.

To go back to the place you marked, just press **Ctrl+G**, click on **Bookmark**, and choose that bookmark's name.

Select Text before You Set a Bookmark

If you select text before you make a Bookmark, that text will be selected again when you use the Bookmark to find it. This is a slick little trick to use if you're copying or cutting text in different locations because your selection appears, ready for you to use.

Going Back to Where You Were

If all you need to do is get back to where you were before, don't bother with a Bookmark. Just press **Shift+F5**. See the tricks and traps for using it earlier in this chapter.

Using Annotations As Post-It Notes

Another hidden trick in Word is using its Annotations feature as Post-It notes to remind yourself of something, or to insert on-screen comments for other readers of your documents. Just press **Alt+Ctrl+A** or choose **Annotation** from the **Insert** menu (**Alt**, **i**, **a**), type your note (see Figure 2.8) and click on **Close** to close the window.

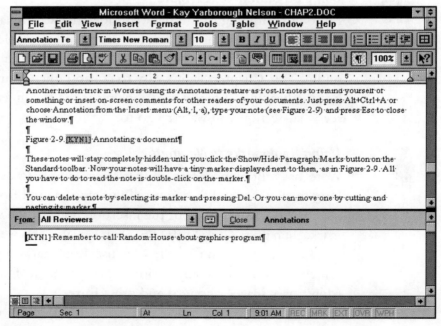

Figure 2.8   **Annotating a document**

These notes stay completely hidden until you click the **Show/Hide Paragraph Marks** button on the **Standard** toolbar. Now your notes will have a tiny marker displayed next to them, as shown in Figure 2.8. All you have to do to read the note is double-click on the marker. Annotations may be printed by choosing **Options** from the **Print** menu, and checking the **Annotations** dialog box.

You can delete a note by selecting its marker and pressing **Del**. You can move one by cutting and pasting its marker.

Select Text before Annotating It

If you select text before you annotate it, Word highlights it later when you're looking at the annotation, so that you can easily see exactly what it was that you annotated. If you want to select that text so you can edit it, just press **Alt+F11**.

Hidden Text

You can hide any text that you don't want to have printed with your document. This is another easy way to make notes or comments in a document, because the "hidden" text is visible on the screen, with a dotted underline under it (Figure 2.9).

Using Hidden Text

To hide text you've selected, press **Ctrl+D** to open the Font dialog box; then check the **Hidden** box. You can also hide selected text with the shortcut **Ctrl+Shift+H**. To make hidden text back into "normal" text again, select it and press **Ctrl+Spacebar**.

Hidden text won't be printed unless you click on the **Options** button in the **Print** dialog box (see Figure 2.10) and check **Hidden Text**.

If you're not sure whether hidden text will be printed or not, here's a quick way to tell: Switch to Print Preview (**Alt, f, v**). If you can see the hidden text in this view, it *will* be printed along with the rest of your document. If you can't see it, it won't be printed. Use the Print Options dialog box to control whether it will be printed or not.

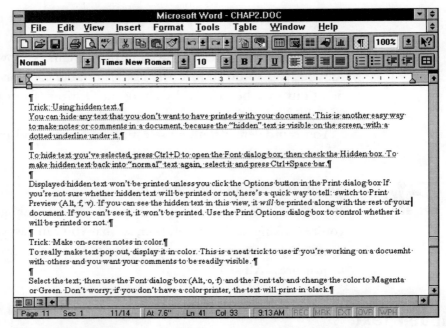

Figure 2.9 Hidden text is displayed with a dotted underline.

Make On-Screen Notes in Color

To really make notes on the screen pop out, display them in color. This is a neat trick to use if you're working on a document with others and

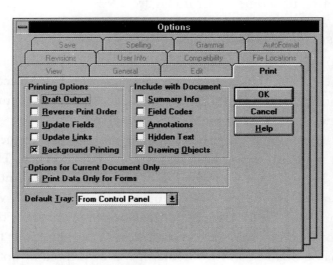

Figure 2.10 The Print Options dialog box

you want your comments to be readily visible when you pass the document around for review.

Select the text, then open the **Font** dialog box (**Alt, o, f**), select the **Font** tab, and change the color to Magenta or Green. Don't worry; if you don't have a color printer, the text will print in black.

Tricks for Search and Replace

You can use the search feature to locate character formatting, such as italics, boldface, 12-point type, and so forth. For example, you can search for all the occurrences of 12-point Helvetica bold in your text, or any other combination of character formatting.

Search for Character Formatting

Click on the **Format** button in either the **Find** or **Replace** dialog box, choose **Font**, and then select the combination of character formatting you want to search for (Figure 2.11). Here, double-spaced Courier is being replaced with single-spaced Helvetica.

Searching for Special Characters

You can search for (and usually replace) special characters by choosing from the **Special** pop-up list on the **Find** and **Replace** menus (Figure 2.12). There are also keyboard shortcuts that let you bypass using this list:

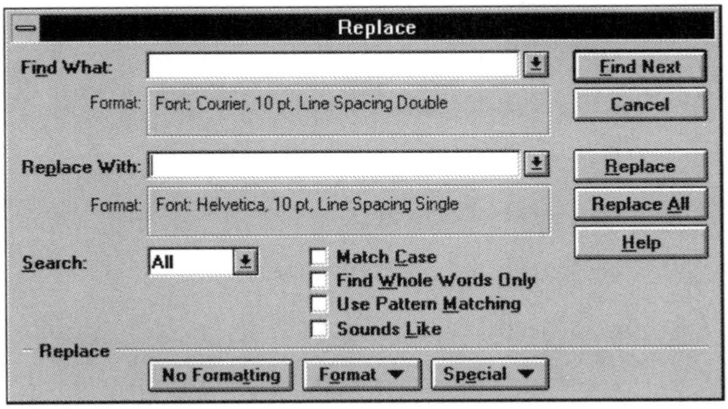

Figure 2.11 Choosing character formatting to search for

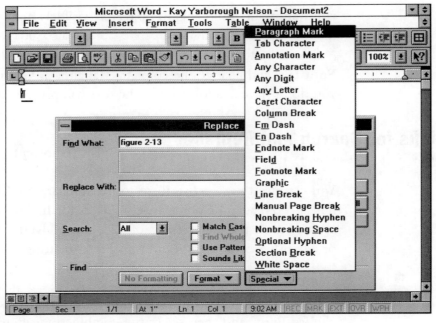

Figure 2.12   Searching for special characters

^~	To search for a nonbreaking hyphen
^+	To search for an en dash
^=	To search for an em dash
^f	To search for a footnote
^e	To search for an endnote
^p	To search for a paragraph mark
^g	To search for a graphic
^l	To search for a line break
^t	To search for a tab
^^	To search for a caret
^?	To search for any character
^#	To search for any digit
^$	To search for any letter

Apply the regular keyboard shortcuts—**Ctrl+B**, **Ctrl+I**, and so on—to the text you've put in the Find What dialog box to search for bold, italics, etc.

To see a list of all the codes for special characters, click the **Help** button on the **Standard** toolbar and then type special characters.

Replace Has Its Own Keyboard Shortcut

If you know you want to replace, use the shortcut **Ctrl+H** instead of **Ctrl+F** for Find. You'll get the Replace dialog box.

Reformatting with the Replace Function

Word lets you search for styles, so you can replace one style with another or even remove all instances of a style from a document. Use **Replace** (**Alt e, e**) and click on the **Format** button when the insertion point is in the **Find What** box. Pick the style you want to delete and then click on **Replace All**.

Replace Text with the Contents of the Clipboard

Here's a neat slick trick: To replace what you're searching for with the contents of the Clipboard, type ^c in the **Replace With** box, or select **Clipboard Contents** from the **Special** drop-down list. Normally, you can replace only 255 characters, but this trick lets you replace with whatever's in the Clipboard, no matter how long it is.

Repeating Searches

Sometimes that big Find dialog box gets in your way. To search again for something without reopening the Find dialog box, just press **Shift+F4**. It's much faster and neater than reopening the dialog box.

Click the **Down arrow** next to the **Find What** box to search for any of the last four things you previously searched for so that you don't have to type them again.

Not Sure of the Spelling?

Word gives you two ways of searching for words whose spelling you're not sure of. You can check either **Use Pattern Matching** or **Sounds Like** in the **Find** or **Replace** dialog boxes.

If you use pattern matching, you can use wildcard characters to represent the parts of the word you're not sure about. For example, to search for *receive* if you're not sure whether it's spelled *recieve* or *receive*, enter **rec*ve** in the Find What box. The asterisk (*****) matches any number of characters or none at all, and the question mark (**?**) matches any one character or none at all. So you could also enter **rec??ve** to search for the two missing letters.

Another example: If you want to search for a company name that's something like *Industrial* or *Industries* or *Independent*, but you can remember only part of it, try searching for *Ind**.

If you use **Sounds Like**, you can enter guess-type spellings like *fearomoan* to have Word find *pheromone*.

Replace/Search Not Working?

Sometimes you don't get what you want when you replace something with something else, or search for something. This maddening condition can be caused by several different factors, the most common of which is that you haven't entered the Find What text correctly. Another thing that can cause a problem is that you may have had some text selected before beginning the search. If that's the case, the replacement works only within that selection. This is very subtle, and you may not notice it.

Also check to see that you haven't checked Match Case and Whole Word in the Replace (or Search) dialog box. Sometimes you're not trying to match the a word or phrase exactly, but with those boxes checked, Word uses only what matches exactly.

One last thing to check: Make sure you're not searching for text that has special formatting, such as boldface or italics. You should see any formatting that's being searched for right there in the Find or Replace dialog box, under Find What. Choose the **No Formatting** button if you see any formatting reported there.

Search for a Unique Word

Try to keep the search pattern as unique as you can. If you search for a common word like *the* or *also,* you're guaranteed to find a lot of them, which just slows down the search process.

Undoing a Search and Replace

If you mistakenly replace all the occurrences of something with something you didn't intend, you can Undo the search-and-replace operation by pressing **Ctrl+Z** (or choosing **Undo** from the **Edit** menu) as soon as the operation is over.

If you do something else, such as reformatting a paragraph or deleting a word, before you use Undo, *that* operation is the one that will be undone, not your search-and-replacement, if you press **Ctrl+Z**. Instead, click on the **Undo** button on the **Standard** toolbar and pick the action you want undone. Word remembers 100 of them.

Replacing Straight Quotes with Curly Quotes

Curly quotes, sometimes called smart quotes, are those like the ones used in this book. They look much more professional in your documents than regular straight quotation marks.

The simplest way to use curly quotes is to use the **AutoFormat** tab in the **Options** dialog box from the **Tools** menu, and check the **Straight Quotes with Smart Quotes** box. Word now replaces quotes as you type them.

If you've turned off that feature, though, you can search for straight quotes and replace them with smart quotes by using the Replace command.

1. Turn on the **Straight Quotes to Smart Quotes** feature in the **Options** dialog box, as in the previous paragraph.

2. Press **Ctrl+H** for Replace and type straight quotes in the **Find What** and **Replace With** boxes.

3. Click on **Replace All**, and Word replaces all the straight quotes with curly ones.

What Next?

· ·

After typing, formatting is the most time-consuming chore in any word processing program. Word has more formatting tricks than you'd ever believe, and lots of them are in Chapters 3 and 4.

Chapter 3

• •

Formatting Tricks

WORD IS FULL OF FORMATTING TRICKS AND SHORTCUTS—in fact, there are usually several different ways to do just about anything you want to do. Instead of covering *all* the different ways to accomplish a task, this chapter will show you some of the slickest tricks for using the Formatting toolbar and the ruler for formatting characters, formatting paragraphs, and creating lists. As usual, we'll start by looking at the keyboard shortcuts, which are usually the fastest method.

Clearing Formatting Changes

Sometimes it's easier just to start all over again, especially if you've made text into a combination of formats. To clear all character formatting from selected text, press **Ctrl+Spacebar**.

Copying and Pasting Formatting

If you need to copy formatting (without copying the text it has been applied to) use this trick: Select the text that has the format you want and then press **Ctrl+Shift+C**. Then highlight the text you want the

61

Keyboard Shortcuts for Formatting
Use that Ctrl key! It gives you all sorts of shortcuts for formatting text without reaching for the mouse. These are some of the easy Control key shortcuts for formatting characters:

Ctrl+B	Turns on **bold**
Ctrl+I	Turns on *italics*
Ctrl+U	Turns on <u>underlining</u>
Ctrl+Shift+D	Turns on <u>double underlining</u>
Ctrl+=	Turns on subscripting
Ctrl+Shift+=	Turns on superscripting
Ctrl+Shift+K	Turns on SMALL CAPS
Ctrl+Shift+A	Turns on ALL CAPS

Select the text you want to apply the format to and press the Ctrl key combination to turn it on. To remove the formatting, use that same Ctrl key combination again; they're toggles.

formatting applied to, and press **Ctrl+Shift+V**. These are easy to re-member, since Ctrl+C copies text and Ctrl+V pastes it.

You can also copy formatting by selecting the formatted text, then clicking on the **Format Painter** button on the **Standard** toolbar, and then selecting the text you want that formatting applied to.

Changing the Default Font Quickly

If you want to change the preset font Word uses for any new document, use this slick trick. Make all the changes you want (font, size, boldface, and so on) and then choose **Font** from the **Format** menu (**Alt**, **o**, **f**), or click the right mouse button and choose **Font**, or press **Ctrl+D**. Then just click the Default button, and you'll be asked if you want to change the Normal template. Say Yes.

Changing Type Size Quickly

You don't need to use the Font dialog box or the Formatting toolbar to change font sizes. Use these handy shortcuts instead:

Ctrl+Shift+>	To go to the next larger size in that font
Ctrl+Shift+<	To go to the next smaller size in that font
Ctrl+]	To increase point size by one point
Ctrl+[	To decrease point size by one point

Checking Character Formatting

If you want to see exactly what formatting is being applied to text, just press **Shift+F1** or click on the **Help** button on the **Standard** toolbar. Then click on the text whose formatting you want to check and you'll see a box showing what formats are in effect. To turn it off, press **Esc** or click on the **Help** button again.

Character Formatting from A to Z

Just so you won't get lost in the font maze, there are a few terms you should be familiar with. First, there are two kinds of fonts: proportional and nonproportional. With nonproportional fonts, such as Courier (the one that looks like typewriter type), each character takes up the same amount of space, whether it's an *m* or an *i*. In a proportional font, each letter takes up a different amount of space—look at the type in this book, and you'll see that an *i* takes up much less space than an *m* or a *w*. For professional-looking documents, use proportional fonts rather than Courier. Word's factory-set default font is Times, which is a proportional font.

There are two kinds of proportional fonts: serif and sans serif. Sans serif fonts are the ones without the little finished endings (called serifs) that appear at the tops, bottoms, and ends of letters. Serif fonts, like the text in the body of this book (and the text on your screen, if you haven't changed Word's default font), have serifs on the characters. You may want to use a sans serif font for headings, and a serif font for the main body text, because serif fonts are generally easier to read. Word's default set-up uses a sans serif font (Arial) for first- and second-level headings, and a serif font (Times) for third-level headings.

The size of a font (any kind of font, unless you're using a dot-matrix printer) is measured in points (pt). A point is approximately $1/72$ inch.

Most text faces are 10 or 12 points; headings are usually 14 or 16 points. Word allows you to use fonts as small as 4 points and as large as 127 points.

A font's point size is measured from the bottoms of its descenders (the bottoms of letters like *g* and *j*) to the tops of its ascenders (the tops of letters like *t* and *l*). The height of the body of a lower case letter is called the font's x-height.

Line spacing (or leading) refers to the amount of space between the lines of text. Technically, it's the vertical distance from the baseline (the invisible line on which the text rests) of one line of text to the baseline of the next line of text. In its default setting, Word calculates line spacing automatically (usually based on the point size of the font you're using) and just asks you what kind of line spacing you want to use (single, double, line-and-a-half, and so on). As you'll see in this chapter, you can use the Paragraph dialog box to choose Exactly or At Least, which give you more control over the amount of space you want between lines.

Tricks for Using the Formatting Toolbar

The Formatting toolbar (called the Ribbon in earlier versions of Word) is another handy way to apply formatting to text (see Figure 3.1). Sometimes it's easier to click in the Formatting toolbar with the mouse than to use a keyboard shortcut.

You can drag the Formatting toolbar (or any toolbar, for that matter) over to the right side of the screen to get it out of your way (see Figure 3.2; notice that the style and font boxes change to icons), or you can change it to a floating toolbar by double-clicking on a blank space in it. To change it back, double-click in it again.

Tricks for Changing Fonts

Quick Font Changes

To change fonts quickly, press **Shift+Ctrl+F**, highlight the font box in the toolbar, type in the name of the font you want to switch to, and

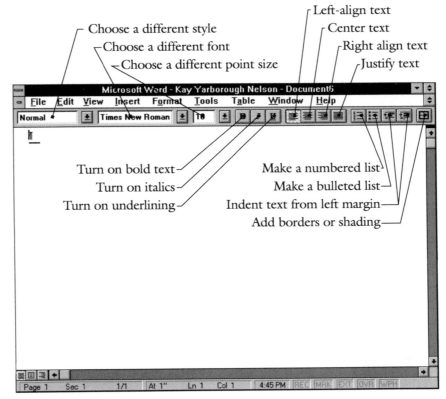

Figure 3.1 The Formatting toolbar

press **Enter**. (Note that this isn't the sort of list where you can type one letter to go straight to that alphabetical part of the list; you must type in the entire name, making sure it is spelled correctly.) You can also click on the arrow button to the right of the font box (or press an **Up** or **Down arrow** key) to display the drop-down font list, use the mouse or the arrow keys to highlight the name of the font you want, and press **Enter**. If you have a large number of fonts, you'll have to scroll through the list.

A Shortcut to Bring Up the Font Dialog Box

A neat shortcut to bring up the Font dialog box is **Ctrl+D**. It's a good one to remember.

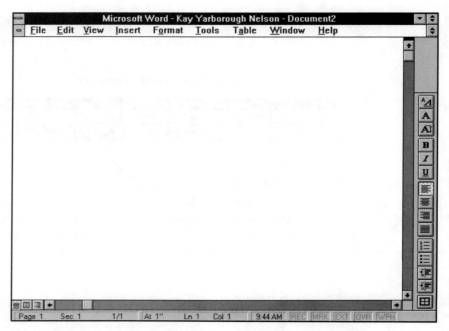

Figure 3.2   The Formatting toolbar displayed on the right side of
the screen

Changing Fonts for an Entire Document

You don't need to scroll laboriously through an entire document whose
body text font you want to change in order to select it. Simply press
Ctrl+A (or choose **Select All** from the **Edit** menu); then change the
font.

Ctrl+A Won't Select Footnotes, Headers, or Footers

Changing the font after selecting the entire document using **Ctrl+A**
or **Select All** does *not* change the font for headers, footers, and footnotes. To change the font for those elements, change their style. If
you need to change the font for footers, for example, change the
Footer style. (See Chapter 4 to learn more about headers and
footers.)

Superscript and Subscript

Here are a couple of subtle points about super- and subscripts. Normally when you change text to superscript or subscript, Word raises or lowers text by 3 points. You can change this amount by using the **Font** dialog box (**Ctrl+D**), checking **Superscript** or **Subscript** (whichever one you want to apply), and clicking the **Character Spacing** tab (Figure 3.3) Click on the menu next to Position and select **Raised** or **Lowered**, then enter the number of points you want to raise or lower the text by in the **By** box.

Changing Letterspacing

You can also change letterspacing in the Character Spacing dialog box to get some of the fancy type effects that are seen so often nowadays. Select the text you want to apply the effect to; then choose **Font** from the **Format** menu and click on the **Character Spacing** tab. In the **Spacing** box (which controls *letter* spacing, not *line* spacing), choose **Expanded** or **Condensed** from the drop-down list.

Click in the **By** box and change the amount by which the letters are spaced. You'll need to experiment (watch the Preview box) with different spacing for some of the popular effects, such as widely spaced capital letters:

K A Y   N E L S O N

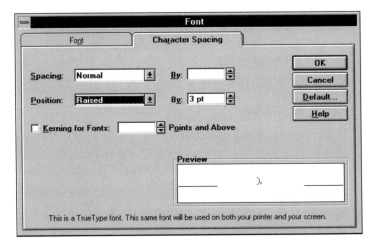

Figure 3.3 Adjusting character spacing

Instantly Switching Case

Use the shortcut **Shift+F3** to change the case of text you've selected. You can quickly toggle between ALL CAPS, Caps And Lowercase, or all lowercase. You saw this trick in Chapter 2, but it's also handy for formatting.

Multiple Formats

Here's a trap you should be aware of: Blank boxes in a dialog box can indicate multiple formats. If you select a portion of text that has more than one character format applied to it—such as different point sizes, fonts, or line spacing—the various formatting dialog boxes may show you blank or dimmed boxes. So a blank box doesn't mean formatting hasn't been used—it may mean that several formats are in effect in the text you selected. To check which formats are being used, see the trick "Checking Character Formatting" earlier in this chapter.

Ruler Tricks

Normally, Word displays a ruler (see Figure 3.4) at the top of the screen, but you can turn it off if you want more screen real estate for your documents. Choose **Ruler** from the **View** menu (**Alt**, **v**, **r**).

The ruler is very handy for changing indents, margins, and setting tabs. Combine using it with a few slick keyboard shortcuts, and you're really in the formatting business.

Using the Rulers

A horizontal ruler is displayed in normal view if you turn it on from the View menu. In Page Layout and Print Preview views, a vertical ruler is also displayed.

While in Print Preview or Page Layout view, it's easy to use the horizontal and vertical rulers together to change margins and adjust the placement of graphics (see Figure 3.5).

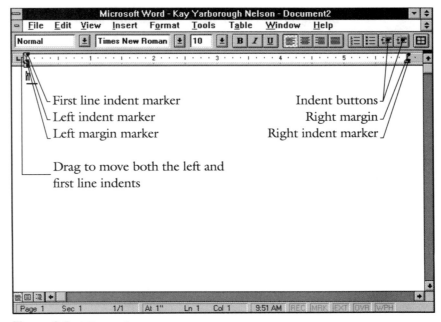

Figure 3.4 The ruler

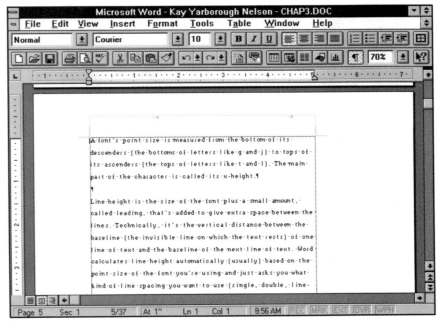

Figure 3.5 The vertical ruler appears in page layout view.

Changing to Picas, Centimeters, or Points

Normally, the ruler is displayed in inches. If you'd rather use picas, centimeters, or points, choose **Options** from the **Tools** menu (**Alt, t, o**) and click on the **General** tab. In the dialog box (see Figure 3.6), choose a different unit of measure from the **Measurement Units** box.

Changing Margins

Drag the right or left margin marker on the ruler to change margins. Press **Alt** as you drag to display the measurements as you adjust the margin marker.

You can also use the **Page Setup** dialog box to adjust margins exactly. Choose **Page Setup** from the **File** menu and click on the **Margins** tab. Or use this handy shortcut: Double-click at the far-right end of the ruler, in the blank space before the scroll arrow.

Creating Hanging Indents Quickly

To create a hanging indent, press **Ctrl+T** when the insertion point is anywhere in the paragraph. Hanging indents look like the next paragraph, and they're often used in lists such as bibliographies. You can

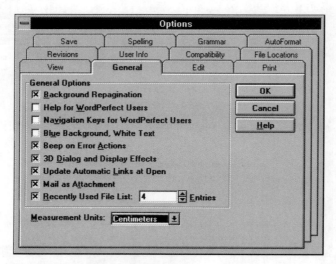

Figure 3.6 **Changing units of measurement in the General Preferences dialog box**

adjust the amount of the outdent in the **Paragraph** dialog box, off the **Format** menu. Choose **Hanging** under **Special** and adjust the amount.

This paragraph is an example of a hanging indent. As you can see, the first line "hangs" out farther left than the rest of the paragraph.

Creating Indents Quickly

To indent a paragraph one tab stop, press **Ctrl+M** with the insertion point anywhere in the paragraph. Press it twice to indent two tab stops. Press **Ctrl+Shift+M** to reset a paragraph to the previous tab stop.

You can also use the **Formatting** toolbar's **Indent** buttons to indent paragraphs using the mouse.

To take out any formatting you've applied directly to a paragraph, press **Ctrl+Q**.

Using the Ruler to Create Indents

You can drag the symbols on the ruler to create indents. Think of the symbols on the ruler as the settings on a typewriter (if you can remember a typewriter). The top and bottom symbols move independently of each other. Try dragging them, and you'll see.

Drag the top downward-pointing triangle to indent the first line of a paragraph. Drag the triangular symbols on the bottom to make a new left indent. Drag the right indent symbol at the far right of the ruler to make a new right indent. (See Figure 3.7.)

If you need precise indents, use the **Paragraph** dialog box (Figure 3.8). Click with the right mouse button and choose **Paragraph** to open this dialog box quickly.

Indent Several Paragraphs at Once

Just select all the paragraphs you want to indent and then click on one of the **Indent** buttons. It's much faster than indenting paragraphs one by one.

To indent *all* the paragraphs in a document, use a style. See Chapter 8, "All Sorts of Slick Tricks."

Figure 3.7 The indent and margin symbols on the ruler

Clearing All Tab Stops

Believe me, it's easier to clear all the tab stops and then set new ones. Otherwise, you get confused about which tab stops are in effect. Instead of dragging tab markers off the ruler one by one, here's a quick way to clear all tab stops: Double-click on any tab marker to bring up

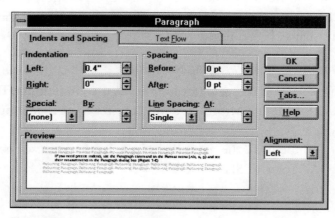

Figure 3.8 Changing paragraph settings in the Paragraph dialog box

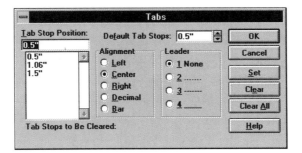

Figure 3.9 Setting tabs in the Tabs dialog box

the **Tabs** dialog box (Figure 3.9). Click on **Clear All**, and it's done. Now you can use the ruler to reset tabs.

Clearing the Default Tabs

Even if you choose **Clear All** in the **Tabs** dialog box, the default tabs will still be there. You can change the default tab spacing, though, by setting it to 5.9" (if your right margin is at 6") to clear all tabs, for all practical purposes. If you try to set the tab spacing to the same as the right margin, Word complains and refuses to let you do it.

Using the Tabs Dialog Box

If you're setting more than just one or two tabs for a bit of quick formatting in a paragraph, use the Tabs dialog box instead of clicking on the ruler. That's where you can clear all tabs at once, set evenly spaced tabs, clear tabs, and choose a leader character to use with tabs.

Double-click on any tab marker for a shortcut to the Tabs dialog box.

To set evenly spaced tabs, click next to **Default Tab Stops** in the **Tabs** dialog box, and pick the increment by which you want to set tabs. Normally, they are set every 0.5 inches.

You can also set an individual tab by entering its position in the **Tab Stop Position** box. To set another tab, click on **Set** and enter another position. The tabs you set will be added to the list under Tab Stop Position.

Don't Use the Spacebar

Always use the Tab key, the indent commands, or the alignment commands to align or indent text. If you use the spacebar and then change to a different font or font size, or change margins, your alignments will be off, because spaces are different sizes in each font.

When you use the Tab key, Word inserts a nonprinting tab character into your document. Normally, you can't see these characters, but if you click on the **Show/Hide** button on the **Standard** toolbar, you can see them (Figure 3.10).

Once you set tabs, they apply not only to the paragraph you have inserted them into, but also to any new paragraphs you create after that paragraph.

Different Kinds of Tabs

You can set left-aligned tabs, right-aligned tabs, centered tabs, or decimal tabs in Word, with or without leader characters (see Figure 3.11).

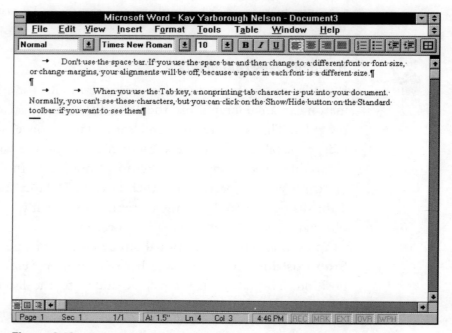

Figure 3.10 Tab characters displayed in a document

PC WORLD

BRITAIN'S
BIGGEST AND
BEST COMPUTER
SUPERSTORE OPENS
IN EDINBURGH

**FROM 9AM
SATURDAY
30TH JULY**

BIG ON CHOICE. BIG ON SERVICE.

PC World, Britain's biggest chain of computer superstores is now coming to Edinburgh.

BIG ON CHOICE

- At PC World you'll find a huge choice of over 5000 computer products – everything from PCs, laser and dot-matrix printers, photocopiers and phones to scanners, soundboards, software, multimedia and mice.

- You'll find all the most famous names to choose from: Apple,

SPECIAL OPENING OFFERS FROM 9AM 30TH JULY

DESKTOP COMPUTERS

DELL PRECISION SI 433 4/170
Inc. Word & Excel Software & SVGA monitor.
£79 ᵉˣ ᵛᵃᵗ – Usually £1119 ⁱⁿᶜ ᵛᵃᵗ **SAVE £1000.** First 1 only

PACKARD BELL CD33S MULTIMEDIA.
Intel 486SX, 33 MHz, 4Mb RAM, 250Mb Hard Disk.
£199 ᵉˣ ᵛᵃᵗ – Usually £1199 ⁱⁿᶜ ᵛᵃᵗ **SAVE £1000.** First 1 only

ADVENT 450D DLC2. 50 MHz, 4Mb RAM, 170Mb HD.
£699 ᵉˣ ᵛᵃᵗ – Usually £849 ⁱⁿᶜ ᵛᵃᵗ **SAVE £150.** First 10 only

OLIVETTI PCS 40 486SX33. 4Mb RAM, 120Mb HD.
£699 ᵉˣ ᵛᵃᵗ – Usually £799 ⁱⁿᶜ ᵛᵃᵗ **SAVE £100.** First 10 only

PACKARD BELL 486SX25. 4Mb RAM, 170Mb HD.
£699 ᵉˣ ᵛᵃᵗ – Usually £799 ⁱⁿᶜ ᵛᵃᵗ **SAVE £100.** First 5 only

DELL OPTIPLEX 425 SL & SVGA Monitor, 4Mb RAM,
SX25 486, 120Mb Hard Drive.
£799 ᵉˣ ᵛᵃᵗ – Usually £1079 ⁱⁿᶜ ᵛᵃᵗ **SAVE OVER £200.** First 10 only

PORTABLES

TOSHIBA 1850 PORTABLE.
120Mb Hard Drive. 4Mb RAM, 25 MHz
£195 ⁱⁿᶜ ᵛᵃᵗ – Usually £795 ⁱⁿᶜ ᵛᵃᵗ **SAVE £600.** First 1 only

HEWLETT-PACKARD OMNIBOOK 486 SLC.
25 MHz, 2Mb RAM, 10Mb Flashcard, Inc. Excel & Word.
£149 ᵉˣ ᵛᵃᵗ – Usually £1099 ⁱⁿᶜ ᵛᵃᵗ **SAVE £950.** First 1 only

TEXAS INSTRUMENTS TRAVELMATE 4000 WIN DX25.
200Mb Hard Drive, 4Mb, Win 3.1 Dos 5.0.
£299 ᵉˣ ᵛᵃᵗ – Usually £1299 ⁱⁿᶜ ᵛᵃᵗ **SAVE £1000.** First 1 only

ZENITH Z325 LP 386SX. 25 MHz Colour Notebook.
£899 ᵉˣ ᵛᵃᵗ – Usually £999 ⁱⁿᶜ ᵛᵃᵗ **SAVE £100.** First 10 only

PRINTERS

OKI OL400EX LASER PRINTER.
£49 ᵉˣ ᵛᵃᵗ – Usually £399 ⁱⁿᶜ ᵛᵃᵗ **SAVE £350.** First 1 only

APPLE STYLEWRITER 2.
£69 ᵉˣ ᵛᵃᵗ – Usually £269 ⁱⁿᶜ ᵛᵃᵗ **SAVE £200.** First 1 only

STAR LC100. Colour Dot Matrix.
£89 ᵉˣ ᵛᵃᵗ – Usually £119 ⁱⁿᶜ ᵛᵃᵗ **SAVE £30.** First 5 only

EPSON LQ100 PRINTER.
24 Pin Dot Matrix – Sheet Feeder 360 DPI.
£99 ᵉˣ ᵛᵃᵗ – Usually £109 ⁱⁿᶜ ᵛᵃᵗ **SAVE £10.** First 10 only

PANASONIC KXP2123. 24 Pin Colour Dot Matrix Printer.
£99 ᵉˣ ᵛᵃᵗ – Usually £149 ⁱⁿᶜ ᵛᵃᵗ **SAVE £50.** First 5 only

CITIZEN ABC & COLOUR KIT.
£149 ᵉˣ ᵛᵃᵗ – Usually £169 ⁱⁿᶜ ᵛᵃᵗ **SAVE £20.** First 10 only

CANON BJ10SX Inkjet **INCLUDES FREE CARTRIDGE**
£119 ᵉˣ ᵛᵃᵗ – Usually £149 ⁱⁿᶜ ᵛᵃᵗ **SAVE £30.** First 5 only

SOFTWARE

WORDSTAR 2 FOR WINDOWS First 15 only
£19.03 ᵉˣ ᵛᵃᵗ – Usually £42.50 ⁱⁿᶜ ᵛᵃᵗ **SAVE OVER £23.**

INTUIT QUICKEN VERSION 3 ACCOUNTING SOFTWARE.
£19.99 ᵉˣ ᵛᵃᵗ – Usually £39.99 ⁱⁿᶜ ᵛᵃᵗ **SAVE £20.** First 30 only

WORDPERFECT INFOCENTRAL.
Personal Information Organiser Software.
£32.50 ᵉˣ ᵛᵃᵗ – Usually £65 ⁱⁿᶜ ᵛᵃᵗ **HALF PRICE** First 20 only

COMPUTER ASSOCIATES SIMPLY BUSINESS.
£19.99 ᵉˣ ᵛᵃᵗ – Usually £83.99 ⁱⁿᶜ ᵛᵃᵗ **SAVE OVER £60.** First 30 only

CLARIS Works with QUICKEN V2 FINANCIAL SOFTWARE.
£74 ᵉˣ ᵛᵃᵗ – Usually £99 ⁱⁿᶜ ᵛᵃᵗ **SAVE £25.** First 10 only

WORDPERFECT 6.0 WORD PROCESSING
SOFTWARE FOR WINDOWS.
£124.50 ᵉˣ ᵛᵃᵗ – Usually £249 ⁱⁿᶜ ᵛᵃᵗ **HALF PRICE** First 10 only

CA CRICKET GRAPH CHARTING SOFTWARE.
£5 ᵉˣ ᵛᵃᵗ – Usually £195 ⁱⁿᶜ ᵛᵃᵗ **SAVE £190.** First 20 only

MICROSOFT SCENES SCREENSAVER.
FREE WITH ANY MICROSOFT PRODUCT PURCHASED.
SAGE MONEYWISE. FREE TO FIRST 50 CUSTOMERS
WHO PURCHASE A PC.

MISCELLANEOUS

INTEL SX2 OVERDRIVE CHIPS First 10 only
£19.99 ᵉˣ ᵛᵃᵗ – RRP £199 ⁱⁿᶜ ᵛᵃᵗ **SAVE £180.**

HAYES SMART MODEM 2400 + QUAD.
Includes error control & data compression
£58 ᵉˣ ᵛᵃᵗ – Usually £189 ⁱⁿᶜ ᵛᵃᵗ **SAVE £130.** First 1 only

REVEAL MEDIA MFX01 MULTIMEDIA EXPLORER PACK.
CD ROM CDs & Speakers, soundcard & headphones.
£189 ᵉˣ ᵛᵃᵗ – Usually £239 ⁱⁿᶜ ᵛᵃᵗ **SAVE £50.** First 10 only

ELDON RUBBERMAID
PC TOOL KIT ACCESSORIES.
£3.95 ᵉˣ ᵛᵃᵗ – Usually £17.95 ⁱⁿᶜ ᵛᵃᵗ **SAVE £14.** First 12 only

ELDON RUBBERMAID. 50 Disk 3½" Disk Boxes
95p ᵉˣ ᵛᵃᵗ – Usually £4.95 ⁱⁿᶜ ᵛᵃᵗ **SAVE £4.** First 60 only

**BUY A PSION 3 OR 3A AND GET A FREE LEATHER CARRY
CASE WORTH £19.99.** First 5 only

PLUS MANY MORE MASSIVE SAVINGS

AVAILABLE IN-STORE – HURRY WHILE STOCKS LAST

Only one of these special offers per customer. No telephone orders
or reservations. Special offers cannot be reserved before 30/7/94.
Dixons Stores Group Ltd. No 504877. 29 Farm St. London W1X 7RD

OPEN 7 DAYS A WEEK

PC WORLD
THE COMPUTER SUPERSTORE

1/17 Glasgow Road, Edinburgh
Telephone 031 334 5953

BIG ON VALUE.

BIG ON SERVICE

- 12 months on-site service included at no extra cost on all Desktop PCs and most printers.
- Enjoy additional peace of mind with the option of extending your warranty for up to five years with Computer Cover.
- Each store has a Technical Centre serviced by our specialists. Our technicians will assist you with upgrades, hardware configuration and software installation.

BIG ON VALUE

- Because we are Britain's Biggest Chain of Computer Superstores our buying power means low prices everyday.

Canon, Compaq, Dell, Epson, Hewlett-Packard, Intel, Lotus, Microsoft, Packard-Bell, Star, Toshiba, and many more beside.

- As well as carrying a massive range of computer products in stock, you can order additional items from our Freephone order service: if it's available, we'll get it for you.
- Instant credit available subject to status, written quotations available on request from: - Dept MK-PCW, 54-58 High Street, Edgware, Middlesex HA8 7EG.

OPENS 30TH JULY AT 9AM

PC WORLD

THE COMPUTER SUPERSTORE

1/17 Glasgow Road, Edinburgh
Telephone 031 334 5953

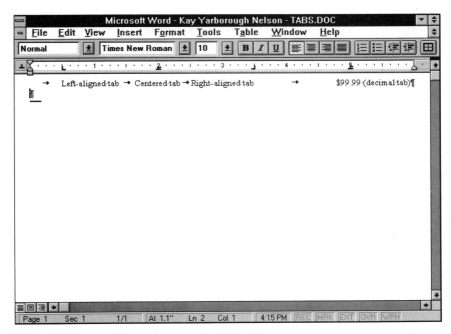

Figure 3.11 Different types of tab indicators

To set a tab, click on the ruler. A left-aligned tab marker appears, because Word sets left-aligned tabs by default.

If you want to set a right-aligned tab, a centered tab, or a decimal tab, click on the **Tab Alignment** button at the far-left side of the ruler. Each time you click, it changes to a different kind of tab. There are four kinds: left-aligned (the L-shaped symbol), centered (the upside-down T), right-aligned (the backward L), and decimal tabs (the upside-down T with a dot). When the Tab Alignment button is showing the type of tab you want to set, just click anywhere in the ruler to set that type of tab.

Using Decimal Tabs

Use decimal tabs if you're typing columns of figures. It's much faster to let Word align columns of numbers on the decimal point automatically than it is for you to try to figure it out yourself. If you're typing columns of dollars and cents, or other numbers that you want to align on the decimal point, set a decimal tab and then type in the figures.

Adding a Leader Character to an Existing Tab

You can easily add a leader character to a tab stop. Open the **Tabs** dialog box, and you'll see a list of tabs that are already set. Select the one you want to add a leader character to, and then pick the leader character you want.

Moving and Removing Tabs

To move a tab stop, just drag it with the mouse. When you release the mouse button, the tab stop will snap to the nearest sixteenth of an inch on the ruler. To remove a tab stop, just drag it completely off the ruler.

Paragraph Styles

You can also put tab settings, as well as other formatting, into paragraph styles, instead of applying formatting feature by feature to different paragraphs. That way, you'll be sure that each particular type of paragraph will have the same formatting. Include tabs, fonts, and point sizes in a paragraph style. (See Chapter 8 for more style tricks.)

A Fast Way to Apply a New Style

Although there are several ways you can apply styles by using the menus, a faster way is to use the keyboard. With the insertion point in the paragraph you want to apply a style to, press **Ctrl+Shift+S**, type the style's name, and press **Enter**.

Formatting Paragraphs

. . . .

One thing you'll need to be aware of in Word—if you aren't already—is that it's a very paragraph-oriented program. Many kinds of formatting affect the whole paragraph, not just the line the insertion point is in. This, of course, presents all kinds of possibilities for some slick tricks (and traps).

The Paragraph Mark

The paragraph mark at the end of the paragraph contains a paragraph's formatting. This really confused me when I first started using Word. It's the paragraph mark being pushed along as you type that contains a paragraph's formatting, and not the one before the beginning of the paragraph, as you might expect. When you press Enter to start a new paragraph, it will have the same format as the paragraph that precedes it. This may be obvious, but it can also be a little confusing. For instance, if you decide to add a new paragraph in the middle of a page, just under a paragraph that's centered and bold, the new paragraph will be centered and bold, too.

Deleting the Paragraph Marker

You can delete a paragraph's formatting if you delete the paragraph marker at the end of the paragraph, so don't delete it unless you're willing for the paragraph's formatting to change. It won't matter if you are permanently deleting the paragraph, but it will if you're cutting the paragraph in order to paste it somewhere else.

Joining Paragraphs

Here's a fine point: To make two adjacent paragraphs into one, just delete the paragraph marker at the end of the first one. The two paragraphs become a single paragraph, which takes on the formatting of the original second paragraph.

Creating a Line Break

Every time you press **Enter**, you create a new paragraph. But if you only want to make a line break, press **Shift+Enter** instead.

Creating a Blank Line

Ctrl+0 (zero) inserts a blank line in front of a paragraph, without inserting a paragraph mark. If you decide you don't want the blank line, press **Ctrl+0** again (or **Ctrl+Z** for Undo).

To put a blank line between several paragraphs at once, select them all, and then press **Ctrl+0**. Instant blank lines!

Shortcuts for Single and Double Spacing

Of course, there also are shortcuts for quickly changing line spacing, and here they are:

Ctrl+1 Changes to single spacing

Ctrl+2 Canges to double spacing

Ctrl+5 Changes to space-and-a-half

You can select text and apply line spacing changes to it, or you can use the Ctrl key shortcuts to change spacing as you're typing text. If you're changing line spacing within a single paragraph only, click anywhere in the paragraph and then change line spacing. You don't have to select the paragraph first.

The Paragraph Shortcut Menu

Just click with the right mouse button in a paragraph, and then choose **Paragraph** to get the **Paragraph** dialog box (see Figure 3.12). You can also reach this dialog box by choosing **Paragraph** from the **Format** menu. Or you can press **Shift+F10** to bring up this shortcut menu if you prefer to use keyboard combinations instead of the mouse.

There are quite a few formats you can apply to paragraphs: indentation, tabs, line spacing, alignment, and so on. If you want to specify line spacing in terms of points, use the Paragraph dialog box.

If you're changing several things at once, it's often faster to use the Paragraph dialog box instead of changing them one by one.

Changing the Spacing between Paragraphs

By adding space between paragraphs, you can easily give your documents an elegant, professional look. Just select the paragraphs whose

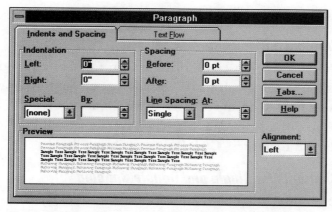

Figure 3.12   The Paragraph dialog box

spacing you want to change (**Ctrl+A** selects the whole document); then click with the right mouse button and choose **Paragraph**. Click on the **Indents and Spacing** tab, and in the **Before** and **After** boxes, choose the spacing you want to add.

For another quick way to adjust spacing between paragraphs, select them and press **Ctrl+0** (zero) to add or delete 12 points of space between them.

More Paragraph Spacing Tricks

Generally, you'll use either Before *or* After paragraph spacing—not both—for regular text paragraphs. However, if you are setting up a style for headings, you'll probably want extra space before the heading, as well as a smaller amount of space following. And if you want to keep extra space around graphics or tables, you can add it both before and after them. That way, if you move them later, the extra space moves along with them.

A good rule to follow is to allow about half a line of extra space, so if you're using 10-point type, and Word is adding 2 points (to make 12 points of leading), put in 6 points of extra space between paragraphs (half a line).

A Hazard of Using the Exactly Setting

If you choose **Exactly** for line spacing in the Paragraph dialog box, Word takes you at your word. If it encounters a character or graphic that is "taller" than the line height you set, the character or graphic will be cut off. If you do this in a document that uses large fonts, super- and subscripts, equations, or graphics, specifying a fixed line spacing can cause problems, because then Word doesn't adjust line spacing for the different elements of text. If you're using any variable-sized text elements in a document, don't specify exact spacing—at least not in those sections of the document. Choose **Auto**, **Single**, **1.5 Lines**, or **At Least** if you want Word to adjust line spacing automatically when it encounters a large character, graphic, equation, or anything else that requires a line height adjustment.

Changing Line Spacing in the Paragraph Dialog Box

When the Line Spacing setting is Auto, Single, 1.5 Lines, Double, or At Least—anything other than Exactly—Word adjusts the line height to fit the largest letter or graphic that it encounters on a line. You can choose At Least or Exactly to have more control over line height.

Quick Alignments

Do you want centered, left-, or right-aligned text? Use these shortcuts:

Ctrl+E   For centered text

Ctrl+L   For left-aligned

Ctrl+R   For right-aligned text

Ctrl+J   For justified text

Again, to change the alignment of a paragraph, just click anywhere in it; you don't have to select it first. This can be a trap: If you want to change the alignment of just one line within a paragraph, you'll find that the entire paragraph changes. You need to press Enter before the line you want to change, to make it a paragraph of its own.

Using Different Alignments in the Same Line

Figuring out how to do this is the sort of thing that can drive you nuts. Say that you want part of a line flush left, another part centered, and a third part flush right. Every time you change the justification, the whole line moves! Here's how to do it:

1. Click in the paragraph with the right mouse button and choose **Paragraph**.
2. Click on the **Indents and Spacing** tab, and click on **Tabs** to bring up the **Tabs** dialog box.
3. Click **Center**, enter 3 in the **Tab Stop Position** box, and click on **Set**.
4. Click on **Right**, enter 6 in the **Tab Stop Position** box, then click on **Set**.
5. Click on **OK** to close the box and return to your document.

Now type the text to be left aligned, press **Tab** and type the text to be centered, then press **Tab** and type the right-aligned text, like this:

Slick Tricks	Chapter 12	Page 50

You don't have to reset tabs after setting up special tabs like this; they'll go back to the default when you move the insertion point out of that paragraph.

An Even Slicker Trick: Use Tables

Another way to get several different alignments on the same text line is to use Word's Tables feature. From the **Table** menu, choose **Insert Table** (**Alt, a, i**). Set up a 3-column, 1-row table; then select the whole table by dragging over it. From the **Format** menu, select **Paragraph** (**Alt, o, p**). Now you have three independent paragraphs in a row. Type text into the cells and use the justification buttons to align each one of them the way you like, or use the shortcuts: **Ctrl+E** (centered), **Ctrl+L** (left aligned), and **Ctrl+R** (right aligned).

Kay Nelson	Computer Books	415/555-7231 phone
Technology Writing	Articles	415/555-9023 fax

Indenting a Paragraph

Here is another slick shortcut: Just press **Ctrl+M** to indent a paragraph.

Justify a Short Line of Text

Word normally doesn't justify the last line of a justified paragraph, nor does it justify a short line that is all by itself. To force it to justify text in a short line, use this trick: Press **Shift+Enter** to end the line, instead of pressing Enter.

Double Indents

You can indent paragraphs from the right margin as well as from the left margin by using the **Paragraph** dialog box to set both a left and a right indent.

Word Remembers Paragraph Formatting

For instance, if you indent a paragraph, the next one you create after pressing Enter will be indented the same way, because Word remembers paragraph formatting. This can be a real timesaver if you're creating several paragraphs that are indented the same way, but it can be frustrating to have to remember to turn the indent off as you type. That's why I usually type a document out and then *go back* and apply formatting to it later.

Margin Release

Remember Margin Release on a typewriter? You can get the same effect—letting the first line of a paragraph stick out into the margin—by entering a negative amount in the **Indentation** box in the **Paragraph** dialog box. What is "outdenting" a line this way good for? Very little, except for numbering paragraphs out in the left margin.

Hanging Indents

Just press **Ctrl+T** to create a hanging indent (see Figure 3.13). Press **Ctrl+T** again to create a deeper indent for the second line of the paragraph. If it's indented too far, press **Ctrl+Shift+T** to decrease the amount of space by which the paragraph is indented. To remove the indent completely, press **Ctrl+Q**. Think of these shortcuts as indenT and **Q**uit.

Starting a Paragraph on a New Page

If you want a paragraph to always start on a new page, click on the **Text Flow** tab and then click on **Page Break Before** in the **Paragraph** dialog box (Figure 3.14). This is a neat trick for forcing new chapters to always begin on new pages, even if you edit the document so heavily that the pagination changes.

Remember that headings are paragraphs, so if you want a first-level heading to always start a new page, you can make the Page Break Before part of that heading's style.

If you're having trouble removing a page break, this setting may be what's preventing you from removing it.

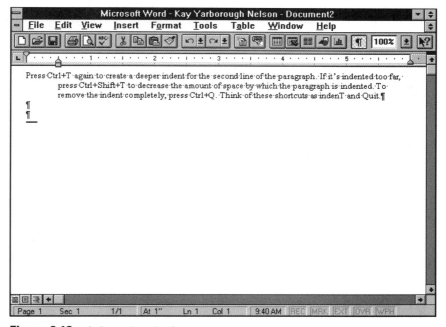

Press·Ctrl+T·again·to·create·a·deeper·indent·for·the·second·line·of·the·paragraph.·If·it's·indented·too·far,·press·Ctrl+Shift+T·to·decrease·the·amount·of·space·by·which·the·paragraph·is·indented.·To·remove·the·indent·completely,·press·Ctrl+Q.·Think·of·these·shortcuts·as·indenT·and·Quit.¶

Figure 3.13 **A hanging indent**

Keeping Paragraphs Together

Sometimes there may be paragraphs that you don't want to be split between two pages. You may have a heading that you want to keep with the paragraph that follows it, for example. Put the insertion point anywhere in the first paragraph; then check **Keep With Next** in the **Text Flow** part of the **Paragraph** dialog box.

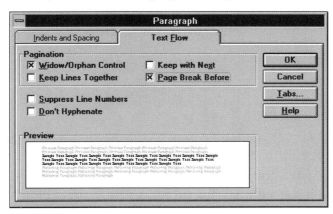

Figure 3.14 **The Text Flow tab in the Paragraph dialog box**

If you want a heading never to be left at the bottom of a page with no text following it, make Keep With Next a part of that heading's style.

Keeping Lists Together
To keep the items in a list together, select them and then click on **Keep Lines Together** in the **3** dialog box.

Preventing Page Breaks in the Middle of a Paragraph
If you don't want a paragraph to be split between pages, check **Keep Lines Together**.

Widows and Orphans
Word automatically checks for widows (single lines at the tops of pages) and orphans (single lines at the bottoms of pages) and moves text so that they will not occur. Check the **Widow/Orphan Control** box in the **Text Flow** tab of the **Paragraph** dialog box.

When to Turn Off Widow/Orphan Control

If you need to create a document that has the same number of lines of text on each page, you should turn off Widow/Orphan Control. When it's checked, Word won't print the first or last line of a paragraph on a page by itself. Instead, it will break the page so that a minimum of two lines of the paragraph move to the next page. If you need an exact number of lines per page, make sure this box isn't checked—it's on by default. It's in the **Paragraph** dialog box, under the **Text Flow** tab.

Forcing a Page Break
Sometimes you want a page to stop at a particular point, and a new page to begin. Just press **Ctrl+Enter** to create a hard page break, or "manual" page break, as you'll sometimes see it called. When in Normal view, you'll see a dotted line on the screen representing the page break (see Figure 3.15).

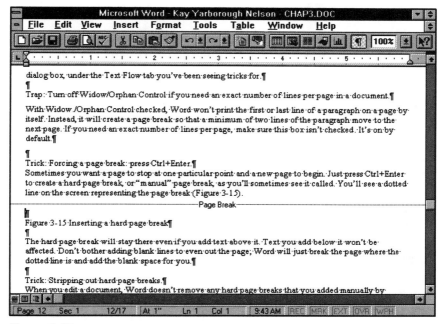

Figure 3.15 **Inserting a hard page break**

The hard page break remains in place even if you add text above it. Any text you add below it won't be affected. Don't try to add blank lines to even out the page; Word just breaks the page where the dotted line is, and adds the blank space for you.

Removing Hard Page Breaks

When you edit a document, Word doesn't remove any hard page breaks that you have added manually by pressing **Ctrl+Enter**. So it's useful to know how to remove any hard (manual) page breaks you don't want from a document.

1 Go to the top of the document (press **Ctrl+Home**).

2 Press **Ctrl+F** for **Find**.

3 Click on **Replace**.

4 Put the insertion point in the **Find What** box, delete any text in the box, and click on **Special**; then choose **Manual Page Break**.

⑤ Leave the Replace With box blank, or delete anything it contains.

⑥ Click on **Replace All** to strip all manual page breaks out of your document, or click on **Replace** to take them out one by one.

Magic Reformatting

Here's a neat trick: Highlight the first word in a paragraph and then format it (or format several paragraphs). Then select any other text, and press **F4** to format them in the same way. You can think of **F4** as the "Same" key; it formats one paragraph the same as another.

Copying Formatting

Here's another slick trick for making one paragraph use the same format as another. Select the text that is formatted the way you want it. Be sure to select the paragraph symbol—otherwise, you'll just copy the character formatting, such as bold, underlining, and so on. Press **Ctrl+Shift+C**; then select the text you want to reformat and press **Ctrl+Shift+V**.

You can also use the Format Painter button on the Standard toolbar. Select the text that is formatted the way you want it; then click on the **Format Painter** button (the one that looks like a paintbrush). The pointer changes to a paintbrush with an I-beam. Now, just select the text you want to be reformatted.

If you want to apply the copied formatting in several different places, double-click on the **Format Painter** button. The pointer remains a paintbrush with an I-beam until you press **Esc** or click on the **Format Painter** button again, so you can keep on selecting text and applying the copied formatting to it.

Removing ALL Formatting

If you've got a paragraph from Hell—one that you can't get back the way it was originally, no matter what you do—try this trick: Highlight the paragraph and press **Ctrl+Spacebar**. If that doesn't make it do what you want, it should at least remove the character formatting. Then you can copy the formatting from another paragraph to the paragraph (as in the previous trick) to align it, indent it, or whatever you want.

Changing the Default Paragraph Format

If you don't like the style Word uses for paragraphs—single spacing, left alignment—it's easy to change it:

1 Select any paragraph in the document.

2 Press **Shift** and select **Body Text** from the **Style** box on the **Formatting** toolbar.

3 Change the format to whatever you want—double spacing, centered alignment, or whatever you prefer.

4 Click on the **Style** box again; then press **Enter** and click on **OK**.

Using Borders and Shading with Paragraphs

For a very slick-looking document, apply borders and shading to selected paragraphs to really make them stand out. It's easy to create those fancy "pull quotes" that you often see in magazines by using this technique.

If you're going to do this, just click on the **Borders** button on the **Formatting** toolbar, and the **Borders** toolbar appears (see Figure 3.16).

If you need more choices than the Borders toolbar displays, use the **Format** menu's **Borders and Shading** command.

To add a border, select the paragraph(s) first; then click on the button with the type of border you want on the **Borders** toolbar. To remove all the borders you've applied, click on the button at the far-right of the border selections.

You can also put borders around graphics and cells in tables—not just paragraphs.

Putting Several Paragraphs within the Same Border

You can struggle for hours trying to figure out how to get three or four separate paragraphs into one box, or you can use this slick trick: Select the paragraphs, copy them, and paste them into a one-row, one-column table. Then put a border around that table.

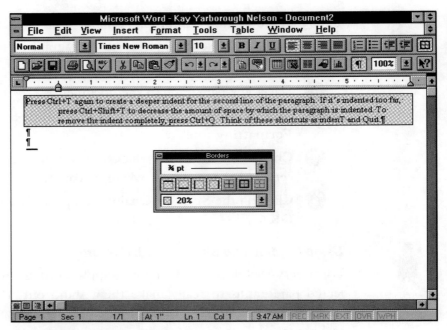

Figure 3.16 A floating Borders toolbar

Keeping Bordered Paragraphs on the Same Page

If you've applied borders to several paragraphs, chances are that you'll want to keep them together on the same page. To stop paragraphs from breaking across pages:

1 Select the paragraphs.

2 Click the right mouse button.

3 Choose **Paragraph.**

4 Click on the **Text Flow** tab.

5 Check the **Keep with Next** box.

Tricks for Special Symbols

• •

The tricks for using special and hidden symbols described in this section will give your documents a professional touch.

Nonbreaking Spaces

A nonbreaking space does what its name says: It stops two words from being broken at the end of a line. For example, if you want to keep a date like February 16, 1995 all on the same line, put the insertion point between February and 16 and press **Ctrl+Shift+Spacebar**. Then do the same between the comma and 1995. On the screen, that nonbreaking space looks like a tiny degree sign (see Figure 3.17).

You can also do this with names, forcing first names, initials, and last names to stay on one line. This adds a subtle but very professional touch to your documents.

Stop Compound Words from Breaking

Have you even been thrown by a line that starts out "-in-law" or with another partially hyphenated word? To force words like mother-in-law to stay all together on one line, use nonbreaking hyphens *instead* of regular hyphens. This is another subtle, professional trick. To create a nonbreaking hyphen, press **Ctrl+Shift+hyphen**.

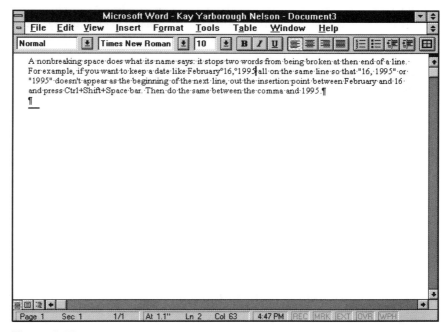

Figure 3.17 **Using nonbreaking spaces**

Other Professional Formatting Touches

Use only one space between sentences, not two. Using two spaces is a holdover from typewriter days. Word automatically adjusts spaces between sentences for you.

Use italics, and not underlines, for book, newspaper, and magazine titles. Underlining is another typewriter relic, since typewriters didn't have italics.

Using Special Dashes

While we're on the subject of professional-looking documents, you should be aware that there are different kinds of dashes. A hyphen is the smallest, and it looks like this: great-granddaughter. You get a hyphen when you press the hyphen key (the one next to the zero). An en dash is a slightly larger dash, and it's used to indicate a range of numbers, such as pages 33–35 or 1945–46. An em dash is a long dash—like this one. It's kind of tacky to keep using typewriter-like dashes--like these-- on your expensive computer.

There are a couple of different ways to place these symbols in your documents. The first, using the Symbol command, is best if you use these characters only rarely. The second, using AutoCorrect, is best if you use these characters a lot.

Inserting Symbols Using the Symbol Command

There's a **Symbol** command on the **Insert** menu (**Alt, i, s**). When you choose it, you'll see a dialog box with all the symbols that are available in the symbol font you are using (Figure 3.18). Just double-click on a symbol to insert it in your document.

If you think you'll be using that symbol often, you can assign it to a shortcut key. From the same menu as above (**Alt, i, s**) click on the **Shortcut Key**. To assign the symbol to a key combination, press the key combination you want to use in the **Press New Shortcut Key** box; then click on **Assign**.

Using Typesetter's Quotes

Instead of using the straight quotation marks you get when you press the " key next to the Enter key, use typesetter's (curly) quotes. From

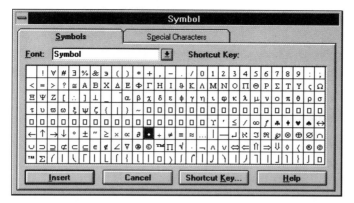

Figure 3.18 **Inserting a symbol with the Symbol dialog box**

the **Tools** menu, choose **AutoCorrect** (**Alt, t, a**). Check the **Change 'Straight Quotes' to 'Smart Quotes'** option, and Word will insert curly quotes—single or double, opening or closing quotes.

Using AutoCorrect to Insert Special Symbols

You can also use Word's AutoCorrect feature to automatically insert em dashes and other special symbols. Here's how to do it for an em dash; use the same procedure for any other special symbols you need:

1. Choose **AutoCorrect** from the **Tools** menu (**Alt, t, a**).
2. In the **Replace** box, type -- (two hyphens with no space).
3. In the **With** box, press **Num Lock**; then press **Alt+Ctrl+Num** – (the minus sign on the numeric keypad).
4. Check the **Replace Text as You Type** box.
5. Choose OK.

Be sure to say Yes when you quit Word and it asks you whether you want to save changes to the global template; that way, you'll be able to have em dashes (or whatever special character you set up) inserted in all your documents as you type.

Now you can type -- and Word converts your ugly double dashes into elegant em dashes as you go along.

To get the keyboard shortcuts for other special symbols, see the next trick.

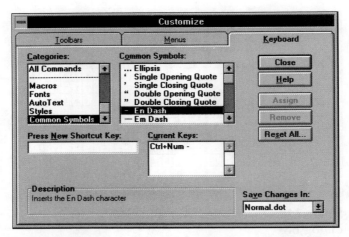

Figure 3.19 Checking the built-in symbol shortcut keys

Built-In Shortcuts for Common Symbols

Word has slick built-in shortcuts for inserting most common special symbols. The real trick is finding out what these shortcut keys are. To do that, choose **Customize** from the **Tools** menu (**Alt, t, c**) and select the **Keyboard** tab. Under **Categories**, choose **Common Symbols** (see Figure 3.19). Now, click on any symbol you want to use and make a note of which keyboard shortcut is already assigned to it!

Using AutoFormat to Insert Special Characters

There are even easier built-in shortcuts for many special symbols, and AutoFormat can take care of them for you.

Word has built-in shortcuts for inserting curly quotes (" "), trademark symbols (™), registration mark symbols (®), and copyright symbols (©). To use them, open the **Options** dialog box (**Alt, t, o**), choose the **AutoFormat** tab, and check (or uncheck) the ones you want (see Figure 3.20).

Then, when you use the AutoFormat feature, Word converts straight quotes to curly quotes, C to ©, R to ®, and TM to ™.

For more tricks for using the amazing AutoFormat feature, turn to Chapter 8.

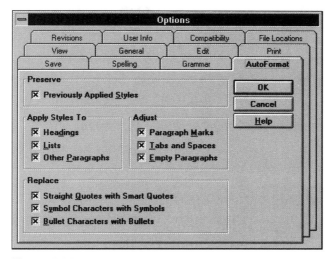

Figure 3.20 Setting AutoFormat options

Creating Lists

· ·

If you have lists in your documents, use Word's automatic features to number them or use bullets with them. That way, if you edit a document heavily and move items around, your numbering will always stay in sequence.

If you want a numbered or bulleted list, just click on the icon on the **Formatting** toolbar. There are many slick tricks you can use with lists, though, and you'll see them in this section.

Creating a Numbered List

All you need to do to create a numbered list is click on the **Numbered List** icon in the **Formatting** toolbar, and then type the item for the list. This is by far the fastest and easiest way to create a numbered list.

You can also just type your list items or paragraphs, and then go back later and number them. Put the insertion point anywhere in a paragraph before you click on the icon, and Word numbers the paragraph. If the preceding paragraph is also numbered, Word will number the current paragraph with the next sequential number. You can even select several paragraphs and Word automatically numbers them for you when you click on the icon on the toolbar.

Stop Numbering

After you've started a bulleted or numbered list, Word keeps right on creating a new item each time you press Enter. Pressing Esc doesn't turn off this feature. Instead, just click on the **Bullets and Numbering** icon on the **Formatting** toolbar again. That will turn it off.

Restarting Numbering within a Document

But what if you want to start numbering with a different number in another part of the document? No problem.

1. Click in your text with the right mouse button.
2. Choose **Bullets and Numbering** from the **Format** menu.
3. Click on the **Numbered** tab.
4. Click on **Modify**.
5. Enter the number you want to start with in the **Start At** box (Figure 3.21).

Bulleted Lists

Do you want bullets or diamonds instead of numbers? Click on the **Bullets** icon in the **Formatting** toolbar to get bulleted lists instead of numbered lists. To change the style of bullet used, go to the **Bullets and Numbering** dialog box (**Alt, o, n**), or right-click, choose Bullets and Numbering, and then click on the **Bulleted** tab. Choose the type of bullet you want.

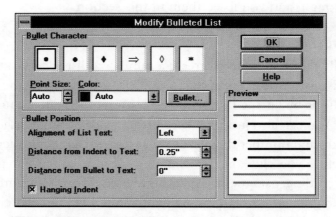

Figure 3.21   The Modify Bulleted List dialog box lets you restart numbering.

Using Different Symbols As Bullets

You can choose a symbol other than the default styles offered. From the **Format** menu choose **Bullets and Numbering (Alt, o, n)**. Select **Bulleted** and then click **Modify**. Click on Bullet, and you'll see the Symbol dialog box showing all the symbols available in the Symbol font. Just double-click on the symbol that you want. To use symbols from a different font, pick that font from the drop-down list next to the **Symbols From** box.

You can also change the size of the bullet you select. The standard bullets are 10, 12, 14, and 18 points. Just type in the different size in the **Point Size** box in the **Modify Bullet List** dialog box.

Switching from Numbers to Bullets, and Vice Versa

If you've started out using numbers and then decide you'd rather use bullets, you can switch from one to the other without doing the whole thing over. Select the paragraphs and click on the **Bullets** button on the **Formatting** toolbar. To switch from bullets to numbers, click on the **Numbering** button. That's all you have to do.

The List Shortcut Menus

To display a shortcut menu for lists, put the insertion point anywhere in a list and press the right mouse button. You'll get a menu (see Figure 3.22) that lets you switch to different bullets, skip numbering, stop numbering, switch fonts, and format your lists.

Interrupting a List

Here's a neat slick trick to use when you need to interrupt a list with text and then resume the list later. Just put the insertion point in the list at the point where you want to break it. Now, press the right mouse button and choose **Stop Numbering**. To restart the numbering, click the right mouse button, choose **Bullets and Numbering**, **Numbered**, and **Modify**. Type in the correct number in the **Start At** box.

Removing a Bullet (or Number) from a List Item

Say that you decide a list item really shouldn't be in the list after all but should be regular text. But you can't delete the formatting without deleting the text. Use this trick to remove the bullet or number only.

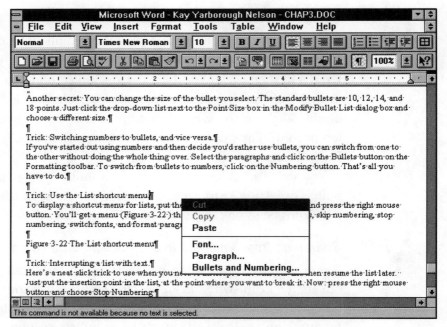

Figure 3.22 **A partial List shortcut menu**

Select the list item; then click on the **Bullets** or **Numbering** button on the **Formatting** toolbar. That will remove the bullet or number but leave the text intact.

Creating an Outline

If you need to create a short outline list in Word, it's almost as easy as creating a list. Click with the right mouse button and choose **Bullets and Numbering**; then click the **Multilevel** tab (Figure 3.23). Pick the style you want to use and click on OK; then go ahead and type your list.

Don't confuse this feature with Word's Outline feature, which lets you structure your whole document as an outline and edit it by rearranging its sections. You'll find tricks for that in Chapter 8.

Quickly Creating Multilevel Lists

Try this slick trick: Type all your list items at the same level in a multi-level list, pressing **Enter** after each one. Then go back and demote the items in the list to the appropriate level by selecting it and using the

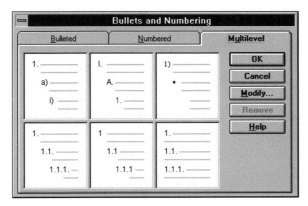

Figure 3.23 Choosing a multilevel list style

keyboard shortcuts **Alt+Shift+Right arrow.** You can use **Alt+Shift+Left arrow** to increase an item's position in the list if you demote it too far.

What Next?

There are lots more formatting tricks in Word. We haven't even begun to scratch the surface yet. The next chapter has all kinds of tricks you can use to format pages.

Chapter 4

. . . .

More Formatting Tricks

IF YOU DIDN'T GET ENOUGH FORMATTING TRICKS in Chapter 3, here's another chapter full of them. The tricks in this chapter will help you format entire documents in Word—changing margins, using text columns, creating banner heads, and such.

Page Formatting Tricks

. . . .

Word has lots of slick tricks for setting up pages the way you want them. In this section, you'll find tips for things like changing all the margins at once, switching to a different paper size, and using headers and footers.

Changing All the Margins at Once
If you're just changing the right or left margin, you can do that with the margin markers on the ruler (switch to print preview or page layout

view). But if you want to change top, bottom, right, and left margins all at once, double-click on a blank part of the ruler and click the **Margins** tab. You can also choose **Page Setup** from The **File** menu (**Alt, f, u**). You'll get the dialog box shown in Figure 4.1.

As you can see, the factory set 1" top and bottom margins and 1.25" right and left margins. Usually, these settings are just fine.

Changing the Default Margin Settings

If for some reason the factory margin settings aren't just fine (see the preceding trick), you can change them to what you want. After you set new margins by using the **Page Setup** dialog box, just click the **Default** button and say **Yes** to the question about whether you want to save the changes in the default template. From then on, each new document you create will use your new margin settings, but documents you've already created will use the old margin settings.

Printing on Both Sides of the Paper?

Word can figure out the margins for you. If you're going to print your document two-sided—on both sides of the paper—check the **Mirror Margins** box in the **Page Setup** dialog box. Word then automatically adjusts the margins on facing pages so that the inside margins (gutters) and outside margins are the same widths.

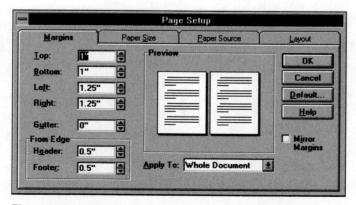

Figure 4.1 Changing page margins in the Page Setup dialog box

Use a Gutter Margin for Bound Documents

If you're working on a document that's going to be side-stapled or spiral-bound, click **Facing Pages**. If your document is more than 30 pages or so, specify a gutter margin, too, so that your readers won't have to crack the binding to read what's down in the gutter. The gutter is the inside margin (see Figure 4.2). Depending on the length of your document and the kind of binding you're going to use, it's often a good idea to make this margin wider. If you specify a 0.25" gutter margin, a quarter-inch will be added to the right margin on even-numbered (left-hand) pages and to the left margin on odd-numbered (right-hand) pages so that text doesn't disappear down into the space between pages.

Anchoring the First or Last Lines of Text

Word changes the top and bottom margin settings when you're using headers and footers so that long headers (several lines of text) don't

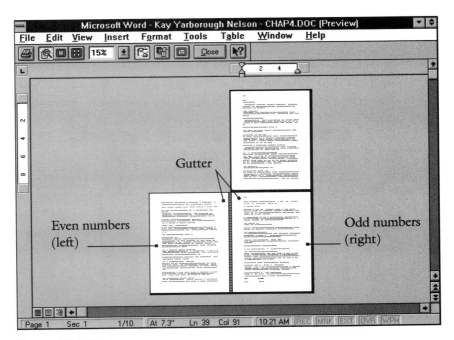

Figure 4.2 Facing pages

push *up* and off the edge of the page into empty space. It does this by pushing the text lines *down* in the case of headers; of course, with a footer, everything's reversed, so the text lines will be pushed *up*. Anyway, it changes the margins for the body (text part) of your document. If you don't want this to happen—normally, you do—you can force Word to keep that margin where you say it should be by entering a minus before the page size in the **Page Setup** dialog box. For example, if you want the first line of text to start at the one-inch mark from the top of the paper, no matter what, enter −1 in the Top margin box.

This may wind up being a trap, though, if you forget that you did it, and then use long headers and footers.

Apply Page Setup Changes to Only Part of a Document

You can make Page Setup changes that apply to just part of a document. If you want your Page Setup changes to apply just to the document from the insertion point forward, choose **This Point Forward** from the pop-up list beside the Apply To label in the **Page Setup** dialog box.

Print Large Tables in Landscape Orientation

To change from Portrait to Landscape orientation, click the **Paper Size** tab in the Page Setup dialog box (**Alt, f, v**). You'll see the dialog box shown in Figure 4.3. Then click **Landscape** under Orientation. If you have a big table that you're trying to get all on one page, try changing to Landscape for just that page and see if your table will fit.

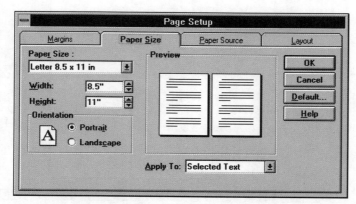

Figure 4.3 The Paper Size tab in the Page Setup dialog box

Changing Paper Size

If you have anything other than 8½ by 11-inch paper loaded in your printer, you'll need to change the paper size. You can choose from a variety of paper sizes from the pop-up list under Paper Size. A4 is a popular European paper size, and B5 is popular in Japan. To specify your own paper size, choose **Custom** in the **Page Setup** dialog box and enter a new width and height. (Don't bother doing this for an envelope! Use the **Envelopes And Labels** command on the **Tools** menu instead!). When you change paper sizes, Word automatically reformats your document for the new paper size.

Keep Letterhead in One Tray and Blank Paper in the Other

Click the **Paper Source** tab if you're lucky enough to have two paper trays attached to your printer. You can keep your letterhead or cover sheet stock in one and regular blank paper in the other. Select the upper tray (holding letterhead) for the first page and the default tray for other pages.

   If you don't have two paper trays, choose **Manual** for the first page, and Word prompts you to insert a letterhead sheet when you go to print the document.

Turn Off Background Repagination to Speed Up Word

Normally, Word figures out the pagination of your document as you type, even if you change fonts, line spacing, margins, and so forth. If you're working on a document that has lots of graphics or large tables, however, repaginating in the background can slow Word down. You can turn off background repagination by choosing **Options** from the **Tools** menu, selecting the **General** tab, and unchecking the **Background Repagination** box.

   Background repagination can't be turned off for Print Preview and Page Layout views, but you may notice that Word is zippier in other views if you turn it off. Keep it on if Word isn't slow on your system, though, so that you can use other features that depend on pagination, such as Go To (F5).

Use Vertical Centering for Title Pages and Cover Sheets

Word has a Vertical Alignment command in the Page Setup dialog box that's ideal for cover sheets and title pages where you want the text centered vertically on the page. You can also use it for short notes and letters that don't fill a whole page, instead of putting a bunch of hard returns at the top of the page and then having to look at Print Preview to see if you guessed right.

Using Headers and Footers

A *header* is text that appears at the top of each page, and a *footer* is text that appears at the bottom. Strictly speaking, they don't appear on "each page" but on pages that you specify. You can have different headers and footers on odd and even pages, or a different one on the first page of your document. You can even have a header and a footer on the same page.

To create a header or footer, choose **Header and Footer** from the **View** menu (**Alt, v, h**). (You'd think this command would be on the Format menu, but it's not; it's on the View menu.) The Header and Footer toolbar appears, and you'll be in Page Layout view, ready to create a header (see Figure 4.4). If you want a footer instead, click on the **Switch Between Header and Footer** button.

You can also use this trick to switch between headers and footers—just double-click in the area you want to switch to. Click in the footer area to switch to a footer, for example. You'll probably have to scroll the page to see the footer area if you're looking at a header.

Aligning Text in Headers and Footers

The header and footer window comes with built-in tabs so that you don't have to think about choosing centered or right alignment. Just type the text you want to be flush left, press **Tab** and type the text you want to be centered, and then press **Tab** and type the text you want to be right aligned.

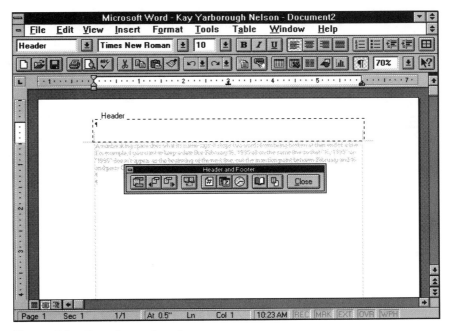

Figure 4.4 Creating a header

Viewing Headers and Footers

You can view just the header or footer without the document text. See the button just to the left of the **Close** button on the **Header and Footer** toolbar? Click on it to view just the header or footer and suppress the text of the document. It's often handy to get a clear view of the header and footer you're creating. Click it again to get the text back.

Putting the Date, Time, and Page Number into Headers and Footers

Just click on the little icons in the **Header and Footer** toolbar to insert the current date, time, or page number.

You can do the same thing by inserting a Date or Time field (see the following tricks).

Inserting Your Name into a Header or Footer

Remember the information about your name and your company name you entered when you installed Word? Word remembers, even if you don't. To have Word insert the information into a header or footer, choose **Field** from the **Insert** menu (**Alt, i, e**), choose **User Information**, and then double-click on **User Name**, and click OK. If you're using summary information in your documents, choosing **Author** also inserts your name. To insert your company name, choose **User Address**.

See Chapter 8 for some background information about using fields in your documents.

Adding the Last-Saved or First-Created Date to a Header or Footer

Do you want a record of when you first created a document in its header or footer? Choose **Field** from the **Insert** menu (**Alt, i, e**) and select the **Date and Time** category. Then choose **Create Date** to insert the date the document was first created, or **Save Date** to insert the date the document was last saved.

Shortcuts for Putting Information into Headers and Footers

You don't have to use the Insert menu to insert fields for different things in your headers and footers. Just press **Ctrl+F9** (Insert Field) and type these field codes into the header or footer itself:

Type	To Insert
author	Your name
filename	The document's file name
numpages	The total number of pages in the document
numwords	The total number of words in the document
createdate	The date the document was created
date	The current date
savedate	The date the document was last saved
useraddress	Your company name or identification
userinitials	Your initials

Putting "Page n of n" Numbering in a Header or Footer

With some word processing programs, getting your pages numbered in the style "Page 4 of 56" is no easy feat. But with Word, it's easy. With the insertion point in the header or footer where you want this text to appear, type Page and press the spacebar. Then insert the page number (click on the **page number** icon). Type a space, type **of**, and type a space. Then choose **Field** from the **Insert** menu, choose **Document Information** as the category, and select **NumPages**.

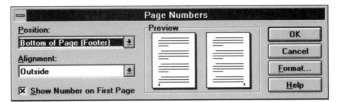

Figure 4.5 Inserting page numbers

Word gives you two simple ways to put page numbers in a document, and each one has its advantages. You've just seen how to put them in headers and footers, which is what you should do if you want fancy text along with the page numbers, such as "Chapter 4, Page 5" or "Page 3 of 48." If you want simple page numbers, use the **Insert Page Number** command on the Insert menu (**Alt, i, u**). You'll see the dialog box shown in Figure 4.5, where you can set up the numbers the way you want them by using the pop-up list under Alignment.

Viewing Headers and Footers to Check Page Number Placement

Word doesn't show page numbers in Normal view, so to check their placement, choose **Header and Footer** from the **View** menu, or use Print Preview.

Formatting Page Numbers

If you want to use roman numerals as page numbers (i, ii, iii) instead of arabic numbers (1, 2, 3), or even use letters (A, B, C, or a, b, c), choose **Page Numbers** from the **Insert** menu (**Alt, i, u**). Click on **Format** and pick the format you want in the **Number Format** box (see Figure 4.6).

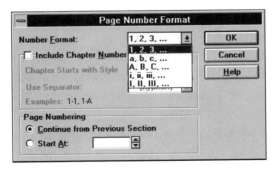

Figure 4.6 Picking a different page number format

If you want page numbers to be in a different font than the text of the document, select **Header and Footer** from the **View** menu. Select the page number and pick a different font from the **Formatting** toolbar. Usually, it's best to pick a smaller size than the document's text.

This trick changes the font for page numbers in the running heads throughout the document, as long as the document has only one section. If your document has more than one section, it's best to change the Page Number style itself to make sure that all the page numbers throughout the document use the same font.

Inserting the Page Number into a Document

While we're on the subject of inserting page numbers, if you want the current page number to appear in the text of your document, use the shortcut **Alt+Shift+P**. You can use this command in the main text of a document, as well as in a header or footer.

Moving Headers and Footers

Normally, Word prints headers and footers ½" from the top or bottom edge of the paper. You can adjust the distance between the header or footer and the edge of the paper by using the **Page Setup** dialog box (**Alt, f, u**) and selecting the **Margins** tab. In the **Header** or **Footer** box, set a different distance in the **From Edge** box.

By the way, you can get to the Page Setup dialog box quickly by just clicking on its button on the **Header and Footer** toolbar. It's the icon that looks like an open book.

If you want to adjust the distance between the header or footer and the text of the document, however, the procedure is a little different. Choose **Header and Footer** from the **View** menu. Then drag the top margin marker down to increase the space between the header and the first line of text, or drag the bottom margin marker up to increase the space between the footer and the last line of text (see Figure 4.7).

Changing the Horizontal Position of a Header or Footer

If you want to have your header or footer centered on the page, click on the alignment buttons on the **Formatting** toolbar; they also align headers and footers.

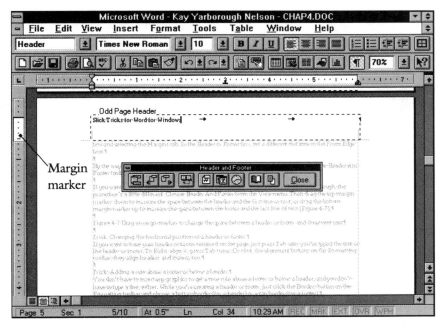

Figure 4.7 Drag a margin marker to change the space between a header or footer and document text.

Adding a Rule Above a Footer or Below a Header

You don't have to insert any graphics to get a nice rule above a footer or below a header, and you don't have to type in a line, either. While you're creating a header or footer, just click the **Borders** button on the **Formatting** toolbar and choose a bottom border (for a header) or a top border (for a footer).

Deleting a Header or Footer

This one can be a trap if you don't know how to do it, but the secret is simple. Act as though you're going to create a new header or footer; choose **Header And Footer** from the **View** menu (**Alt**, **v**, **h**). Select the header or footer you want to delete (if you don't select it first, Word beeps at you and you can't delete it), then press **Backspace** or **Del**. That's all you have to do.

If you've used different headers and footers in the same document, click on the **Show Next** and **Show Previous** buttons on the **Header and Footer** toolbar to make sure you delete them all.

If you've added a rule, as in the preceding trick, the rule may stay there. If it does and you want to remove it, select its paragraph mark and press **Ctrl+Q**.

Using Different Headers and Footers on Different Pages

Putting a book's title on its left-hand pages and the chapter title on its right-hand pages adds a sophisticated touch. Even if you're not writing a book, you can alternate different headers and footers on facing pages. All you have to do is click on the **Page Setup** button on the **Headers and Footers** toolbar (**Alt**, **v**, **h**) while you're creating a header or footer; then click on the **Layout** tab in the **Page Setup** dialog box. Under **Headers and Footers**, check **Different Odd And Even**.

Now, click on the **Show Previous** or **Show Next** buttons on the **Headers and Footers** toolbar and create the header (or footer) you want to have on left-hand (even-numbered) and right-hand (odd-numbered) pages.

Suppressing a Header or Footer on the First Page

Normally, you don't want a header or footer on the first page of a document, such as a chapter opener or business letter. To suppress a header or footer on the first page, go to the beginning of the document with **Ctrl+Home**. Then choose **Header and Footer** from the **View** menu (**Alt**, **v**, **h**). Click on the **Page Setup** button on the **Header and Footer** toolbar; then click on the **Layout** tab. Under **Headers and Footers**, check the **Different First Page** box and click **OK**. Now, here's the trick: Leave the header or footer area completely blank. Go to the next page (click on the **Show Next** button) and create the header or footer you want to have on all the rest of the pages. Finally, click on **Close**.

Aligning Headers and Footers on Facing Pages

It's a professional-looking touch to have headers (or footers) flush left on left-hand pages and flush right on right-hand pages. To get this effect, make sure you've set up your document for facing pages (see the trick "Printing on both sides of the paper?" earlier in this chapter). Then set up your header or footer and check the **Different Odd and Even Pages** box in the **Page Setup** dialog box , as you've just seen. (If the text for the header/footer on odd and even pages is the same, don't check this box.) Now: Locate your right-hand-page header, put the insertion point at the beginning of the text, and click on the **Align Right** icon in the **Formatting** toolbar.

Match Page Numbers in Headers and Footers

If your page numbers in headers and footers aren't matching the real page numbers of your document, try this trick. Select the page number in the header/footer window and press **F9**, the Update Field key.

Be Careful When Changing Headers and Footers

If you edit headers and footers within a section, your changes apply to the whole document. Word uses the headers and footers you set up in the first section of a document in *all* the other sections of the document unless you take an extra step: Click on the **Same As Previous** button on the **Header and Footer** toolbar. This can be confusing, because you *don't* want the new header or footer to be the same as the previous header or footer.

If you haven't set up sections in the document, Word just beeps at you when you try to use this button, so forget about it unless you're using sections with different headers and footers.

Tricks for Sections

If you want to use different headers and footers or margins, change page numbering to a different system and restart with 1 or with a number you specify, or number lines in a document starting with 1 over again, you should set up a section. You may think of a section as several pages long, such as a chapter in a long document, but a section can be just a paragraph or a few lines. And, of course, this lends itself to all sorts of slick tricks.

To start a new section, put the insertion point where you want the section to start, and then choose **Break** from the **Insert** menu (**Alt, i, b**). You'll see the dialog box shown in Figure 4.8; choose one of the options under **Section Breaks** and click on **OK**.

Figure 4.8 The Break dialog box

If you want the section to start on a new page, click on **Next Page**. You can click on **Even Page** or **Odd Page** to specify whether the new page should be even (left-hand, if you're printing both sides) or odd (right-hand). Most things like chapters and title pages always begin on a new right-hand (odd) page. Click on **Continuous** if you want the new section to be on the same page you were on. A section break mark looks like the one shown in Figure 4.9—a double dotted line.

Using a Different Layout for a New Section

Once you've set up a section, you can easily change it to use a different layout, using a different number of text columns, paper size, margins,

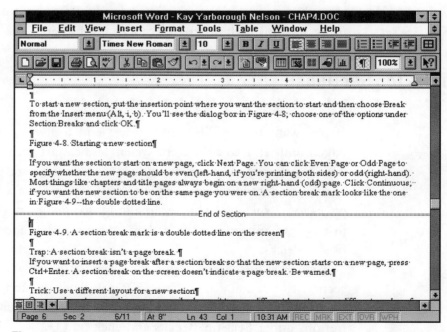

Figure 4.9 A section break mark is a double dotted line on the screen.

page numbering, line numbering, headers and footers, and so on. The changes you make in the new section won't affect preceding sections.

A Section Break Isn't a Page Break

If you want to insert a page break after a section break so that the new section starts on a new page, press **Ctrl+Enter**. Be warned: A section break on the screen doesn't indicate a page break.

Getting Different Numbers of Columns on the Same Page

The preceding trick also allows you to have different numbers of columns on the same page: by setting up a new section and clicking **Continuous** under **Section Breaks** in the **Break** dialog box; then setting up a different number of columns.

Numbering Pages in a Document with Sections

You'll often want to change the starting page number in individual sections of a document. For example, you may want to start each section with a new page 1, or use a page number style such as 2–1 for page 1 of section 2.

To change the starting page number in a section, put the insertion point anywhere in the section; it doesn't have to be at the beginning. Choose **Page Numbers** from the **Insert** menu (**Alt, i, u**), and click on **Format**. Type a new page number in the **Start At** box. Click on **OK** until you get back to your document.

Beware of Page Numbers When Using Sections

Watch out when putting page numbers in headers and footers if you're also using sections. Be aware that a potential trap exists: If you're putting page numbers in a header or footer, you'll need to set up different headers and footers for each section if you want sections numbered differently, instead of sequentially from the first page of the document. See the trap "Be Careful When Changing Headers and Footers" earlier in this chapter.

Using Line Numbers

Line numbers are used in many different types of legal documents, and you'll sometimes see them used in dramatic scripts as well, to help the actors keep track of the lines. If you need to number each line in a document, you'll need to use the **Page Setup** dialog box. Double-click on a blank spot on the ruler to bring it up quickly; then click on the **Layout** tab. Click on the **Line Numbers** button and select the **Add Line Numbering** box (see Figure 4.10).

Starting with a Number Other than One

You can start numbering with a number other than one by entering a different number in the **Start At** box.

To change the distance between text and line numbers, use the **From Text** box. (If you leave **From Text** set to Auto, line numbers are printed 0.25" from the text—out in the margin. If you're using columns, they're printed 0.13" from the text, between the columns.)

In the **Count By** box, type the increment you want if you don't want line numbers printed at every line. For example, to print a number every five lines, type **5**.

Evenly Spaced Lines and Line Numbers

If you want lines and line numbers to be evenly spaced, use the following tricks.

Word normally adjusts line height to accommodate different fonts and point sizes. If you want beautifully, evenly spaced lines and line numbers, use one typeface in one size. Go to the beginning of the document (or wherever line numbering starts), click the right mouse

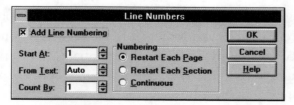

Figure 4.10 Setting up line numbering

button, and choose **Paragraph** to bring up the **Paragraph** dialog box. Under **Line Spacing**, choose **Exactly**; that way, all lines will have the same spacing.

Don't use any of the spacing "before" or "after" options in the Paragraph dialog box, so that all lines will have the same spacing, even between paragraphs.

What Is a "Line?"

Just so you don't go crazy trying to figure this out: Word doesn't count footnotes, tables, footers, or headers as lines.

Suppressing Line Numbers for Certain Paragraphs

If you don't want certain paragraphs to be included in the line count, or if you don't want headings to be numbered, suppress line numbering for those paragraphs.

1. Select the paragraph(s).
2. Choose **Paragraph** from the **Format** menu (**Alt, o, p**).
3. Click on the **Text Flow** tab.
4. Check the **Suppress Line Numbers** box.

Removing Line Numbers

If you later decide that you don't want numbered lines in your document after all, go to the **Page Setup** dialog box (remember the double-click-on-the-ruler trick?), click on the **Layout** tab, click on the **Line Numbers** button, and uncheck the **Add Line Numbering** box. The insertion point can be anywhere in the section that has line numbers.

If you're using line numbers, it's sort of by guess and by golly, since they don't appear on your screen in most views. Use Page Layout view or Print Preview to see line numbers.

Text Column Tricks

"Text columns" in Word means newspaper-style columns. You may have seen these called *snaking* columns, too, because the text flows from the bottom of one column to the top of the next column.

Don't Use Columns

If you want columns or paragraphs to be side by side, such as in a schedule of events, a resume, or a play script, *don't use text columns* and laboriously insert column breaks by hand. Use the **Table** button and set up a table instead. Then just type the text for your columns into the cells. Use no borders, and put the text that is to be side by side into adjacent cells.

Creating a Resume? Use a Wizard.

One common use for text columns is in resumes, so don't waste time with columns if that's what you want; Word has a built-in Resume Wizard. Use it! That's what Wizards are there for.

Open a new document (click the **New Document** button in the **Standard** toolbar, or choose **New** from the **File** menu), and from the **Template** box, select the **Resume Wizard**. If the resume isn't exactly as you want it, you can edit it, but it sure beats creating a resume from scratch.

Type in Text before Changing It to Columns

It's much more efficient to type text and then change it to a column format than to worry about formatting text into columns as you go along.

Creating Columns Quickly

All you need to do to create columns in Word is to click on the **Columns** button on the **Standard** toolbar and then drag to select the number of text columns you want. You'll get columns of equal width. If you want columns that have unequal widths, see the next trick.

Creating Two Columns with Different Widths

To create columns that don't have the same width, choose Columns from the **Format** menu (**Alt, o, c**), set the number of columns you want in the **Number for Columns** box (see Figure 4.11), and then click on **Left** or **Right** under **Presets**. This makes either the left or right column narrower than the other. If you want to specify exact column widths, enter measurements under **Width** and **Spacing**.

That's the easy way for only two columns. If you're using more than two columns and you want them to have different widths, make sure the **Equal Column Width** box in the **Columns** dialog box is unchecked. Then enter measurements for the columns under Width and Spacing.

Changing Column Widths the Easy Way

Go to page layout view and just drag the left or right column markers to change column widths.

A Shortcut to Return Text to One Column

To convert text in multiple columns back to a single one, click on the **Columns** button on the **Standard** toolbar and then click on the first column.

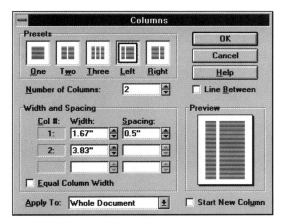

Figure 4.11 Setting column measurements in the Columns dialog box

Editing Columns in Page Layout View

The normal view of a document shows only one column at a time. To see columns side by side, switch to Page Layout view. You may find it easier to edit columns when you can see how they're breaking on the page.

Putting Rules between Columns

Don't struggle with the manual, or do logical things like putting borders around paragraphs, to get rules between your columns. Just check the tiny, often overlooked **Line Between** box in the **Columns** dialog box, and Word automatically inserts rules between text columns for you, as shown in the Preview in Figure 4.12. You won't see them in normal view; use Page Layout view or Print Preview to see the results.

An Easy Way to Use Columns in Part of a Document

If you want to switch between one-column and multicolumn text in a document, just select the text that you want to have in columns. Then apply a column format to that text. Word automatically puts that text into a separate section for you, and you don't have to do anything else.

This is another good reason for typing a document and *then* formatting it.

Getting Columns of Equal Length

Word automatically fills a page of text with columns all the way to the bottom of the page, before switching to the next column. As a result,

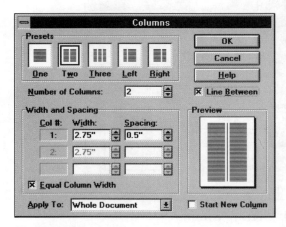

Figure 4.12 Using rules between columns

sometimes the last in a group of columns ends up as one long column down the left side of the page, while you may prefer short, evenly balanced columns *across* the page. With other word processing programs, you may have to use all sorts of tricks, such as creative editing, changing line spacing, and so on, to make columns balance across a page (or to "have equal feet," as you'll sometimes hear). In Word, it's easy—just choose **Break** from the **Insert** menu (**Alt, i, b**) and click on **Continuous** under **Section Breaks**. Word formats the single long column into whatever number of columns you're using and spaces them equally across the a page. (You need to be in Page Layout view to see the results.)

Creating a Banner the Easy Way

If you want a heading that spans a page with columns, as in Figure 4.13, why not do it the slick and easy way? Convert the text to columns; then select the heading, click the **Columns** button on the **Standard** toolbar, and click the first column to convert only the heading to a one-column format.

Forcing a Column to Break Where You Want It To

Isn't it maddening when a column doesn't break the way you want it to at the bottom of a page? Here's a slick trick for forcing a column break: Put the insertion point where you want the column to end. Then press

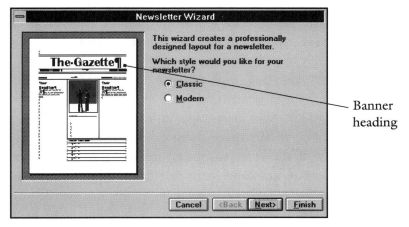

Figure 4.13 Creating a banner heading over columns

Ctrl+Shift+Enter. It's usually best to do this in Page Layout view, where you can see what's happening.

There's also a **Break** command on the **Insert** menu (**Alt, i, b**), but the keyboard shortcut is faster.

Preventing Column Breaks

What if there are two paragraphs that you want to keep together even if Word would normally break them between columns? This can happen, for example, when a heading is near the foot of a column, and you want to make sure that the heading and the following paragraph stay together.

The trick is to use the Paragraph dialog box. Select the first of the two paragraphs that you don't want split apart. Then click with the right mouse button, choose **Paragraph**, click on the **Text Flow** tab, and check the **Keep with Next** box.

Forcing Graphics to Stay with Text in Columns

Sometimes Word may break a column in a way you don't like, because there are graphics inside the column. You can stop it from doing this. Go to Page Layout view and select the graphic that you want to keep anchored to the text just after it. Then click the right mouse button and choose **Paragraph**. Click on the **Text Flow** tab and check the **Keep With Next** box.

Forcing a Page Break in Columns

Do the same thing you'd do to force a page break anywhere else: Press **Ctrl+Enter** where you want the page to break.

Narrow Columns? Reset Paragraph Indents.

Word's default paragraph indents can overpower narrow columns, because they'll make them even narrower. Double-click on the top part of the ruler to open the **Paragraph** dialog box; then set the indent to zero and see if that fixes the problem. If it does, add extra spacing before or after paragraphs instead of using a paragraph indent.

What Next?

· ·

We've covered a lot of formatting tricks in this chapter. In the next chapter, we'll look at tricks for setting up Word to suit your own personal preferences. If you're still hungry for formatting tricks, you'll find more of them in Chapter 8, which covers a variety of topics.

Chapter 5

· ·

Customizing Word for Windows

YOU HAVE CONTROL OVER MOST of the ways Word works, although you may have never taken the time to sit down and adjust it to suit yourself. The tricks in this chapter will show you how to take charge of Word's factory settings (called default settings) and set Word up to work the way you want to work. In addition to setting the program's formatting to suit yourself, you can customize the toolbars, the menus, the keyboard shortcuts, and more.

Changing the Default Font

Tired of seeing the same old font all the time? Word starts out using Times or Times New Roman if one of these fonts is available for the printer you've installed. If it can't find a font of the Times family, it may use Courier, that notorious typewriter-like font, as your default font. If that's the case—or if you don't like Times—it's time to change the default font.

The fastest way to change the default font is to select text that's already in the font you want to switch to; then click the right mouse button, choose **Font**, and click on the **Default** button (Figure 5.1).

If there's no text handy that's already in the font you want, you can click the right mouse button, choose **Font**, pick a new font and point size from the dialog box, and click on the **Default** button. In either case, you'll be asked to confirm that this is what you want to do.

Say **Yes** when you're asked whether you want to change the template when you quit Word, or your default font change won't "stick" and the next time you start Word you'll see Times (or worse, Courier) again.

To change the entire Normal template, see Chapter 8, "All Sorts of Slick Tricks."

Getting More Screen Real Estate

You can suppress the ruler and toolbar(s) to add extra space for displaying text on your screen. You might want to do this if you're settling down for a session of straight typing and you plan to come back to the document and format it later. Or you may want to turn off the rather cluttered upper-screen display if all you're doing is spell-checking or reading through a document.

Word has a handy Full Screen command that will clear the screen for you in a hurry. It's on the **View** menu, and **Alt**, **v**, **u** is its keyboard

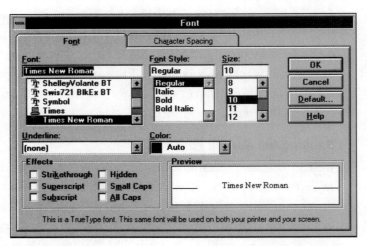

Figure 5.1   The Font dialog box lets you change the default font.

shortcut. There's also a button for it in Print Preview (**Alt f, v**). If you find that you like to see the full screen most of the time, try this slick trick: Go into Print Preview and click on the **Full Screen** button (the one that looks like a tiny screen); then return to your document by clicking on the **Close** button. Now you'll get a **Full Screen** button floating on your screen, which you can click on to return to Normal view.

Turning Off Screen Displays

If you want to suppress any one element, such as the Standard toolbar, you can choose it from the View menu to turn it off. The controls that turn off the ruler and the toolbars are toggles—they're either off or on. If one is on (meaning that the item is being displayed on the screen), there'll be a check mark next to it.

♦ To turn off (or display) the ruler, choose **Ruler** from the **View** menu (**Alt, v, r**).

♦ To turn off (or display) a toolbar, click in any toolbar with the right mouse button to bring up the list of toolbars. Then pick which toolbar you want to turn off or display.

Customizing Toolbars

Those toolbars taking up space on the top of your screen can be customized to suit your heads. Here's how.

Make Your Toolbars Larger

If your toolbar buttons are hard to see, just make them bigger. Choose **Toolbars** from the **View** menu (**Alt, v, t**). Then, in the Toolbars dialog box (Figure 5.2), click **Large Buttons** at the bottom of the dialog box.

Notice that you can also control whether toolbars are displayed in color and whether the ToolTips—the messages that appear when the cursor is over a button—appear.

Moving a Button on a Toolbar

If there's a button you use frequently, consider moving it to an easier-to-reach position on the toolbar. Just press **Alt** and drag it to a new location.

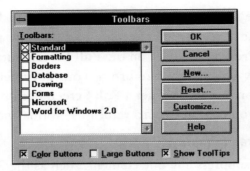

Figure 5.2 Use the Toolbars dialog box to enlarge buttons.

Removing a Button from a Toolbar

You can also remove buttons you never use from a toolbar. Just press **Alt** and drag the button off the toolbar.

Moving and Copying Buttons onto Different Toolbars

Sometimes you may want to put a button on a different toolbar. To move a button from one toolbar to another, just press **Alt** and drag it, with both toolbars displayed. To copy it instead of moving it, press **Alt+Ctrl** and drag.

Restoring a Toolbar

If you change buttons on a toolbar and then decide you don't like the way the toolbar is now set up, use the handy **Reset** button instead of trying to put each button where it was originally. Choose **Toolbars** from the **View** menu, select the toolbar you want to reset, and click **Reset**. Pick the template the changes will apply to and click OK.

Adding a New Button to a Toolbar

You can put any of Word's commands on a toolbar, as a button. It's easy.

1 Display the toolbar you want to add the new button onto.

2 Choose **Customize** from the **Tools** menu.

3 Click on the **Toolbars** tab.

4 Choose the category with the command you want to make into a button. The buttons for that category appear (Figure 5.3).

5 Drag the button you want to add onto the toolbar that's displayed on your screen.

If the command you want to add to a toolbar isn't included in one of the standard categories, choose **All Commands** from the Categories list. Then pick the command you want to add and drag it to the toolbar.

Make Buttons for Single and Double Spacing

You might want to make buttons for switching to single or double spacing. The commands for those are called SpacePara1 and SpacePara2. Here's how to make a double-spacing button:

1 Select **Customize** from the **Tools** menu and click the **Toolbars** tab.

2 Choose **All Commands** under **Categories,** scroll the commands, and locate **SpacePara2.**

3 Drag the command to the **Standard** toolbar.

Making Specialized Toolbars

You can even create a toolbar from scratch if you want to. Here's how to do it:

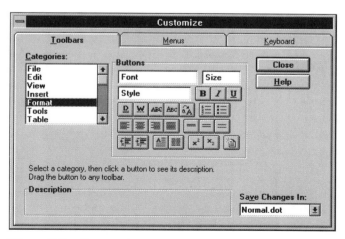

Figure 5.3 Customizing a toolbar

1 Select **New** in the **File** menu, then select the template you want the toolbar to be attached to. Usually, this will be the Normal template.

2 Choose **Toolbars** from the **View** menu.

3 Click **New** and give your new toolbar a name.

4 You'll see a small, empty toolbar. Choose the categories you want from the Customize dialog box and drag buttons over to the empty toolbar.

5 When you're done adding buttons, click on **Close**.

Changing Menus

Word also lets you change its menu system, adding commands you want and deleting those you don't want. To edit the menu system, select the **Customize** command on the **Tools** menu and click the **Menus** tab (Figure 5.4).

Notice the tiny **Save Changes In** box at the bottom-right corner of the Customize dialog box. Make sure it displays Normal.dot if you want the changes you make to menus to be available in all your documents.

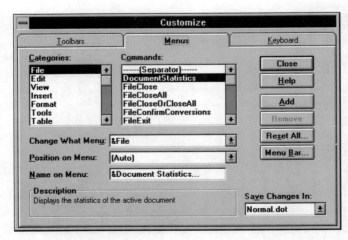

Figure 5.4 The Menus tab in the Customize dialog box

Bypassing the Customize Dialog Box

There's a slick way around using the Customize command. In fact, you can add many commands to menus directly from most dialog boxes. Just open the dialog box and press **Alt+Ctrl+=**. Click once on the item in the dialog box that you want to put on a menu. Choose **Cancel**. Nothing seemed to happen, did it?

But open the menu that normally controls that dialog box (for example, if you added a font, open the Format menu) and you'll see the command you added.

This is a neat way to put a font you use frequently on the Format menu. Press **Alt**, **o**, **f** to go to the Font dialog box, press **Alt+Ctrl+=**, and click on the font's name. Then click on **Cancel**. Now open the **Format** menu and see that the font you added is there.

Adding an Item to a Menu

You can add commands to any of Word's menus, including its shortcut menus. Here's how:

1. Choose **Customize** from the **Tools** menu and click the **Menus** tab.

2. Choose a category and a command, as you've seen in previous tricks.

3. Select the menu you want to change from the **Change What Menu** list.

4. From the **Position on Menu** list, pick the position where you want the command to appear.

5. In the **Name on Menu** box, type the name you want the item to have.

6. Click on **Add** and **Close**.

Assigning Your Own Shortcut Key to a Menu Item

See the ampersands in the boxes in the Customize Menu dialog box? They occur just before the letter that's used as that menu command's shortcut key. All you have to do is type an ampersand in front of the letter you want your menu command to use as a shortcut. Be careful, though: Don't pick a shortcut key that's used for another command on that menu, or Word won't be able to figure out which command to use when you press that shortcut key.

Customizing the Shortcut Menus

It's simple to customize the shortcut menus that appear when you click the right mouse button. Choose **Customize** from the **Tools** menu (**Alt, t, c**); then select the **Menus** tab. Scroll the **Change What Menu** list (Figure 5.5) until you see the commands that have (Shortcut) next to them. Choose a command and click on **Add**. You'll also be able to pick a new position in the list of menu choices.

Renaming a Menu Command

Here's another easy way to customize Word's menus: Rename the commands to suit yourself.

1 Select **Customize** from the **Tools** menu.

2 With the **Menus** tab selected, pick the category and command you want to change, as you've seen in previous tricks.

3 In the **Name On Menu** box, type a new name for the command. Use the ampersand trick (see the trick "Assigning your own shortcut key to a menu item") to give your new command a shortcut key.

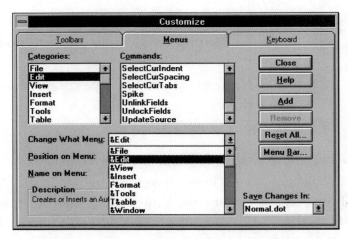

Figure 5.5 Scroll the Change What Menu list to locate the shortcut menus

4 Click on **Rename** and **Close**.

You can't change the names of some of the basic commands, like Exit.

Deleting a Command from a Menu

Ah, here's a slick trick. Just press **Alt+Ctrl+−**, open a menu, and click on the command you want to delete. That's it.

There are a few necessary commands, such as Save and Open, although you can always use their buttons on the toolbar even if you take them off the menus. But, if there's no button for a menu command, consider carefully whether you want to delete it.

To get a command back that you delete by mistake or decide that you really need after all, Select **Customize** from the **Tools** menu and click on **Reset All**.

Renaming a Menu

Word will even let you rename a menu if that's what you want to do.

1 Select **Customize** from the **Tools** menu and click on the **Menus** tab.

2 Click on the **Menu Bar** button to bring up the **Menu Bar** dialog box. In the **Name On Menu Bar** box, type a new name for the menu. Use an ampersand before a letter to set up a shortcut key for that menu (don't use one that's already taken by another menu, though).

3 Choose the menu's name on the **Position On Menu Bar** list.

4 Click on **Rename** and close the dialog boxes.

To get the menus back to their original names, select **Customize** from the **Tools** menu and click on **Reset All**.

Creating a New Menu

You can even create a brand-new menu if you want to (although you can't create a new shortcut menu). To make a new menu, follow these steps:

1 Select **Customize** from the **Tools** menu and click on the **Menus** tab.

2 Click on the **Menu Bar** button that you saw in the previous trick.

3 In the **Name on Menu Bar** box, type a name for your new menu.

4 In the **Position On Menu Bar** box, pick a position for your new menu.

5 Click on the **Add** button, then the **Close** button.

6 Add the menu items you want to have on your new menu by choosing categories and commands from the Customize dialog box, as you saw in the earlier trick "Adding an Item to a Menu."

When you close the dialog box, you'll see your new menu.

You Can Even Delete a Menu

With all this customizing going on, it's logical that Word will let you delete a menu, too. First, select **Customize** from the **Tools** menu and click the **Menus** tab. Then click on the **Menu Bar** button to bring up the **Menu Bar** dialog box. Now, select the menu to be deleted from the **Position On Menu Bar** list and click the **Remove** button.

To get a deleted menu back, select **Customize** from the **Tools** menu, click on the **Menu** tab, and use the **Reset All** button.

Don't Delete the Tools Menu

If you delete the Tools menu, you'll have a hard time choosing Customize from it to get the Customize dialog box, which has the handy Reset All button that lets you restore changes you've made to menus. There is a way around this, but the easiest solution is simply not to delete the Tools menu.

Customizing the Keyboard

There's a Keyboard tab (Figure 5.6) in the Customize dialog box that lets you set up keyboard shortcuts of your own and reassign Word's existing keyboard shortcuts to other combinations. You can assign shortcut keys to AutoText entries, fonts, commands, special characters—all sorts of things—as you'll see in the tricks in this section.

Switching keyboard assignments is another customization job you'll need to explore on your own, because it involves personal preferences. But you can change Word's keyboard assignments to keys you feel more comfortable with and assign shortcuts that your fingers may have already "memorized" from another program.

The basic technique is the same as the one you've seen already—select the command you want and then assign it a key combination.

A Shortcut to the Keyboard Tab

Here's a slick trick: Press **Alt+Ctrl+Keypad+**. Click on a menu item or button. You'll instantly go to the Keyboard tab in the Customize dialog box with that command selected, ready for you to give it a shortcut key combination or reassign the one it already has.

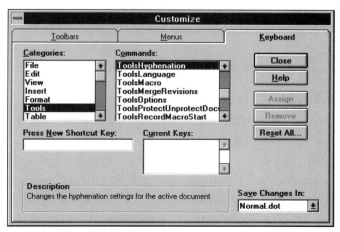

Figure 5.6 **The Keyboard tab in the Customize dialog box**

Assigning a Shortcut Key to a Command

Once you're looking at the Keyboard tab (select **Customize** from the **Tools Menu**), here's the basic procedure you use to assign a shortcut key:

1 Choose a category and a command, as you've seen in previous tricks. Watch the Current Keys box to see if that command already has a shortcut key assigned. You can reassign it if you like.

2 In the **Press New Shortcut Key** box, press the keys you want to use as the new combination. You can use function keys, Ctrl-key combinations, Shift+Ctrl key combinations, Alt+Shift combinations, Alt+Shift+Ctrl combinations, Alt+Ctrl combinations...you get the idea. You can't reassign F1, the universal Windows Help function key, however.

3 Choose the template you want to save the changes in. Usually, you'll leave this as Normal.dot unless you're assigning a shortcut key combination that you want to operate only in a particular specialized template.

4 Click on **Assign** and **Close** the dialog box.

Assigning a Shortcut Key to a Style

When you're creating a new style (select **Style** from the **Format** menu and click the **New** button), there's a **Shortcut Key** button in the **New Style** dialog box. You can click it to go directly to the **Keyboard** tab in the by-now-familiar Customize dialog box and set yourself up a shortcut key for that style.

Removing All Your Shortcut Key Assignments

It's easy to reassign a key combination or two and then decide later that you liked the old way after all. Fortunately, Word has a handy Reset All button on this Keyboard tab, too. Select **Customize** from the **Tools** menu, click on the **Keyboard** tab, then click on the **Reset All** button.

   Use the Remove button to remove a current shortcut assignment. That won't assign it back to the original combination, though. Use Reset All to do that.

Changing How Word Works — The Options Menu

The Options command on the Tools menu brings up a dialog box with several tabs. By clicking on any of the tabs, you can display more dialog boxes that let you customize Word's settings. I'll point out some useful changes you can make, and you can view these dialog boxes on your own to see if there are any other changes you'd like to make.

The View Tab   You can change how you view documents by selecting **Options** from the **Tools** menu and clicking on the **View** tab. You'll get the dialog box shown in Figure 5.7.

Turning Off the Scroll Bars

The box in Figure 5.7 labeled **Window** allows you to turn off the horizontal and vertical scroll bars as well as the status bar. However, it's not usually a good idea to turn them *all* off. If you do away with the vertical scroll bar, you may gain an extra bit of space on the **right** of your screen, but you won't be able to scroll through a document. Most of the time, you can probably do without the horizontal scroll bar at the bottom of the screen, though.

The status bar? It's up to you. If you never look at it, nuke it, too. But it does show page numbers, total pages, and things like that. In addition, it tells you when the Macro Recorder is on, when you've turned on Caps Lock and Num Lock, whether you're in Overtype mode, and so forth. And you can double-click on it to get the Go To dialog box.

Adjusting the Style Area

The style area is a normally invisible area on the left of the screen. Use this trick: When in Normal view, select **Options** from the **Tools** menu, click on the **View** tab, then turn the style area on by setting a width in the box labeled **Style Area Width.** You'll need a width that's wide enough to read style names (look at Figure 5.8). About an inch will do

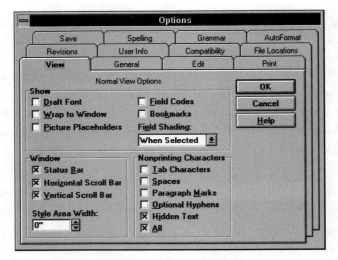

Figure 5.7 Changing View options

if you're using long style names, but you can make the style area as wide as half the screen. Don't worry about guessing the exact width to set; just set any width here (say, 0.5") and then drag the style area splitter bar (the line dividing the style area from the text area in the document window) to accommodate the width of your style names.

To hide the style area, just drag the splitter bar to the right margin.

Turn on Picture Placeholders

When you scroll a document with graphics in it, they will appear and disappear in an annoying fashion as you scroll. Word is doing this deliberately to avoid constantly redrawing the screen. If you turn on Picture Placeholders, you'll just see empty boxes in place of graphics, and you'll scroll much faster, too. Select **Options** from the **Tools** menu, click on the **View** tab, and then click in the box labeled **Picture Placeholders**.

View Field Codes Only When Needed

Field codes are embedded commands you put within your Word documents, and Chapter 8 explains more about them. Press **Shift+F9** to switch between seeing field codes and their results while you're in a document.

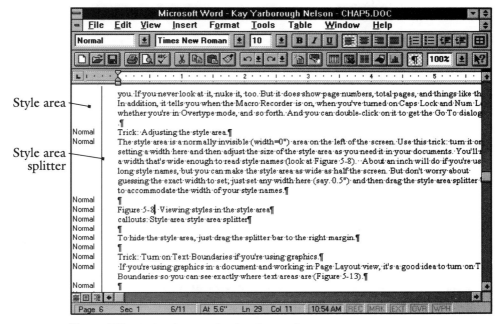

Style area ⟍

Style area splitter ⟍

Figure 5.8 Viewing styles in the style area

Use the Show Nonprinting Characters Button

It's much faster to click the **Show Nonprinting Characters** button at the far-right end of the **Standard** toolbar than it is to select **Options** from the **Tools** menu, click on **View**, and turn nonprinting characters on and off. Use the dialog box only to select which nonprinting characters you want to see, such as only paragraph marks.

The General Tab There are all sorts of ways you can customize Word by selecting **Options** from the **Tools** menu and using the settings under the **General** tab (Figure 5.9). The next few tricks will give you some ideas.

Make Word Look More Like Word for DOS

Want white text on a blue background, like Word for DOS? Many folks find this combination easier to read than Word for Windows' normal "white" screen. Click Blue Background, White Text.

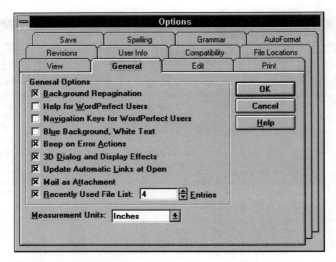

Figure 5.9   The General tab

Customize the Recently Used File List

Normally, Word displays the names of the last four documents you worked with at the bottom of the File menu. You can display as many as nine or as few as none by changing the number next to the **Recently Used File List** label.

The Edit Tab   Use the **Edit** tab to control how Word replaces, selects, or inserts text.

Disable Typing Replaces Selection

Select **Options** from the **Tools** Menu, click on the **Edit** tab, and turn off **Typing Replaces Selection** if it's bothering you. Normally, in a Windows word processor, you can immediately start typing to replace selected text without bothering to delete it first. (You have to delete it first in a DOS word processing program.) This may cause you to make replacements mistakenly or delete text you didn't intend, because your selection is deleted as soon as you type the first new character.

Turn Off Automatic Word Selection

Normally, Word will highlight the entire word when you extend a selection instead of extending the selection only to the letter next to the insertion point. If you'd like to be able to select letter by letter, turn off this feature. Select **Options** from the **Tools** Menu, click on the **Edit** tab, and uncheck the **Automatic Word Selection** box.

Use the Ins Key to Paste

Overtype mode is pretty useless unless you're typing columns of equal-sized numbers. Instead, check the box next to **Use The INS Key For Paste**, and then you can press **Ins** to paste just as though you were pressing **Ctrl+V**.

The Revisions Tab

Use the Revisions tab to control how Word marks deletions and insertions in a document that several people are working on. The settings you choose on the Revisions tab (Figure 5.10) affect how Word marks revisions to a document when you choose **Revisions** from the **Tools** menu (**Alt**, **t**, **v**) and use the **Revisions** dialog box (Figure 5.11).

Change the Marking Method

Normally, Word uses underlining to mark inserted text. You can change it to bold, italics, or double underline if you want, by choosing from the list next to **Mark** under **Inserted Text**.

Use a Different Color for Each Commentator

If several authors are commenting on or revising a document, use a different color to display their markings on the screen. Word is set to do this for you, but it's a new feature in version 6.0, and you may not realize it's there. Word can keep track of as many as eight different authors' comments by color.

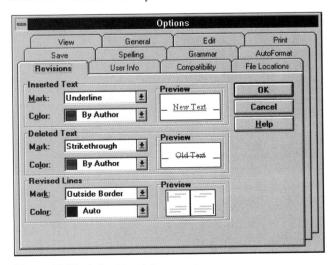

Figure 5.10 The Revisions tab

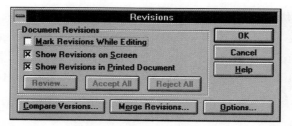

Figure 5.11 Options in the Revisions dialog box

The User Info Tab

The **User Info** tab in the **Options** dialog box (**Alt, t, o**) handles the information you provided when you installed Word (see Figure 5.12)—your name, your initials, and your mailing address if you provided one when you created an envelope. If any of the information you provided changes, you can change it here.

The Compatibility Tab

Use the **Compatibility** tab in the **Options** dialog box (**Alt, t, o**) to set options for converting documents created in other programs. If you use other word processing programs, such as WordPerfect or an earlier version of Word (for Windows, DOS, or the Macintosh), you can fine-tune how Word imports documents created by those programs. Don't bother trying to figure out what each of these options are for! Just pick the other word processing program you use from the list under **Recommended Options For** (Figure 5.13) and see which options Word is

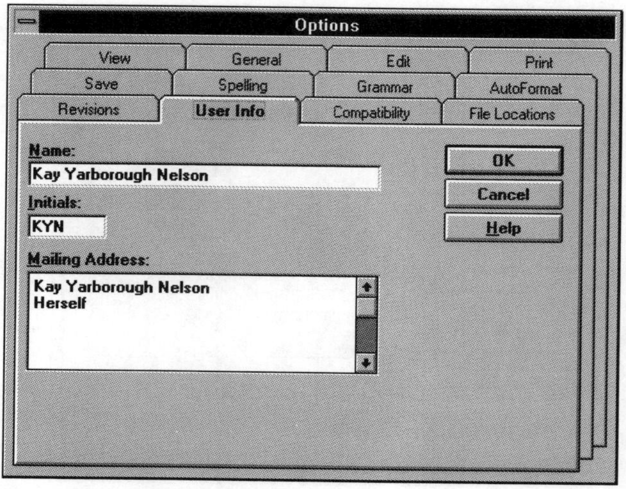

Figure 5.12 The User Info tab

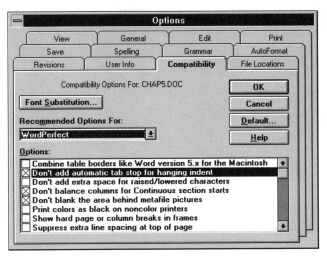

Figure 5.13 Viewing recommendations for
WordPerfect

recommending. Then, if you're still not getting the results you want,
try changing a few of these options.

***The File
Locations Tab***

Set your own preferences for the directories where Word stores files.
The default directory is the directory where Word automatically saves
the documents you create. Normally, it's C:\WINWORD, but saving all
your documents in this directory isn't usually a good idea, because it
gets cluttered with all your templates, Word program files, and such.

Changing the Default Directory

To save documents in a different directory so that only Word program
and template files are in your C:\WINWORD directory, you can enter
a different path when you use the Save As command, but that's a bit
tedious. There's a faster way. If, for example, you want almost all of your
documents to be saved in C:\WINWORD\DOCS\REPORTS (or any
other directory you specify) you can change the default directory. For
the few files that you don't want saved in this directory, you can enter
a path or click to open folders where you want them saved.

To change the default directory, choose **Options** from the **Tools**
menu (**Alt**, **t**, **o**). Click on the **File Locations** tab (Figure 5.14).

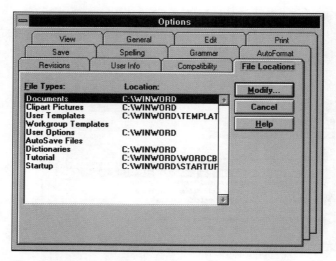

Figure 5.14 The File Locations tab

Choose the **Modify** button and, in the **Modify Location** dialog box (Figure 5.15), select the directory you want to use for storing documents. Then click on **OK** and close.

If that directory doesn't exist, you'll get an "invalid" message. To create the directory, open the directory you want the new directory created *under*, and then click on the **New Folder** button. Enter the name you want the new subdirectory to have.

You might also want to direct backups to the same directory where other programs store their backups. If you crash, you can find backup files from all the programs you've been working on in there. To change the default directory for backups, do this:

1 Choose **Options** from the **Tools** menu (**Alt, t, o**).

2 Click on the **File Locations** tab.

3 Click on **AutoSave Files** and **Modify**.

4 Enter the name of the directory where you want backup files saved, such as C:\BACKUPS.

5 Click on **OK** and **Close**.

Now, if you have a power failure or other problem, you can find your Word backups (automatic saves) in C:\BACKUPS.

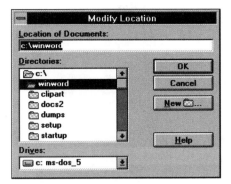

Figure 5.15 Changing the default (working) directory

The Save Tab   You can also get to this dialog box when you click the **Options** button in the **Save As** dialog box.

Options for Saving documents

Save TrueType fonts with a document so that you can display the document on another computer that doesn't have those fonts installed.

The **Save** tab (Figure 5.16) lets you set all sorts of options for saving your documents. One of the slickest tricks you can use, if you know you're going to be taking documents to other people's computers, is to click on the **Embed TrueType Fonts** box so that Word saves the font information along with the document. That way, you won't have to worry about which fonts are installed on the other computer(s) you'll be displaying that document on. Be sure to use only TrueType fonts in the document (the ones with TT next to them in the font list) so that this trick will work!

Creating Backups

Check **Always Create Backup Copy** on the **Save** tab in the **Options** dialog box (**Alt, t, o**) if you need a copy of the *previous* version of your documents. The "backup copy" Word creates is the previous version of your document saved with a .BAK extension. If you anticipate a situation where you might make a mistake—during a round of revisions, for example—and need to restore the previous version of a document, turn this feature on by checking its box.

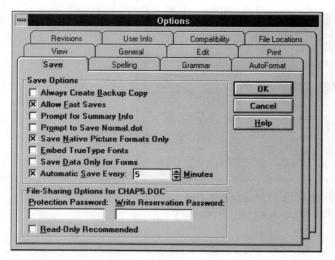

Figure 5.16 The Save tab

Keep the Automatic Save Feature On

Word is preset to save your document every 10 minutes. You can reset this time interval to a period as short as every one minute or as long as every two hours (120 minutes). If the power goes off, Word automatically opens this saved version of your document the next time you start the program (with "Recovered" as part of its name in the title bar), so you should get some of your changes back even if you haven't saved the document manually in awhile. Only the changes you made to the document after the last automatic save will be lost.

You Can't Have Backup Copies and Fast Saves

Fast saves take a lot less time than full saves, because Word saves the complete revised document when it does a full save, and it saves only the changes you've made when it does a fast save. However, backup copies that the program makes automatically (see the sidebar "Safe Saves" in Chapter 1) require full saves. So, if you wonder why the Allow Fast Saves box in the Options dialog box is unchecked when you check Always Create Backup Copy—that's why.

Read-Only Documents

You can protect an important document by making it read-only when you open it. Check the box next to **Read-Only Recommended** on the **Save** tab in the **Options** dialog box (**Alt, t, o**). Now, when you open an important document—one that you normally don't want changed—you'll see a warning message recommending that you open the document as read-only (meaning that you can't save any changes).

The Spelling Tab You can also set spelling options in Word. Do you want to use a different custom dictionary? Or turn off suggested replacements for misspelled words, which makes spell-checking faster? Are you annoyed by always stopping at alphanumeric combinations like F2? Don't want to be bugged with questions about words like RU486? Click on the **Spelling** tab in the **Options** dialog box (**Alt t, o**) shown in Figure 5.17.

Custom Dictionaries

You can change dictionaries, switch to a custom dictionary, or use several dictionaries at once in the **Spelling** tab in the **Options** dialog box (**Alt, t, o**). Select any dictionary listed under **Custom Dictionaries** to use it—you can choose more than one. It's fastest, though, to use the main dictionary only.

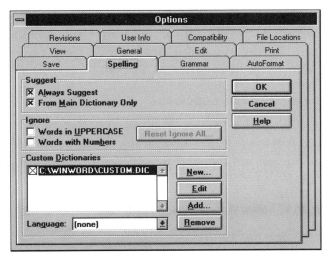

Figure 5.17   **Changing Spelling options**

Helpful Hints for the Speller

Try some of these tricks to speed up spell-checking:

As soon as you see a misspelled word in the Not In Dictionary box, start typing the correctly spelled word.

As soon as you realize you OK'd a word that really was incorrect, click the Undo Last button.

Keep the mouse pointer over the Change All button. You'll be surprised at how many times you've typed a word wrong in the same way. Choosing Change All changes every occurrence of that misspelling in the document, which speeds up spell-checking.

Add word combinations such as Ctrl+F2 to the dictionary so Word won't query you on them again. If you choose Ignore All instead, Word will ask you about them in the next document you check.

Check the spelling of a selected new area if you've already checked the document before. There's no point in checking it all again. Just select the text and press **F7** to start the spell-checking process.

Start checking spelling from anywhere in a document. When Word gets to the end, it will ask you whether you want it to continue at the beginning.

Creating a Custom Dictionary

To create a custom dictionary or to use one that isn't listed in the **Custom Dictionaries** list on the **Spelling** tab, click on **Add**. In the **Add Custom Dictionary** dialog box, type the path to where the dictionary you want to use is stored.

Speeding Up Spell-Checking

You can speed up the process of spell-checking a document by unchecking the **Always Suggest** box on the **Spelling** tab. If you do that, Word won't suggest replacement words. You can just manually correct typos instead.

Keep Your Custom Dictionary Accurate—and Small

Edit your custom dictionary from time to time to get those misspelled words that you added by mistake out of there. Choose **Options** from the **Tools** menu; click on the **Spelling** tab. Choose the custom dictionary

(CUSTOM.DIC) and click on **Edit**. You'll be asked if you want to continue; click on **Yes**. Then edit the list of words to remove any misspellings and save the document.

Keeping your custom dictionary small will also speed up spell-checking.

What to Ignore in a Spell Check

Turn off checking words with numbers in them, or words in UPPERCASE if your documents have these in them. If you have alphanumeric words, such as 4.0C or RU486, in your documents, or words that always appear in ALL CAPS, check those boxes under **Ignore** on the **Spelling** tab in the **Options** dialog box (**Alt, t, o**) so that Word won't ask you about such word patterns when you check spelling.

The Grammar Tab

Use the **Grammar** tab to customize the grammar checker and set the maximum number of words per sentence.

Changing Grammar Tab Options

If you don't like the way Word's grammar checker works, tweak the options on the **Grammar** tab (Figure 5.18) in the **Options** dialog box (**Alt, t, o**). There are all sorts of things that you can change.

Another way to get to this dialog box is to click on **Options** in the **Grammar** dialog box that you see when you choose **Grammar** from the **Tools** menu (**Alt, t, g**).

Under **Use Grammar and Style Rules**, click on the method you want Word to use. **Strictly** really is strict, and it's best for writing where you want to make your most proper impression. Click on **For Business Writing** for a slightly less strict interpretation of what your grade-school teacher taught you (and you forgot). Click on **For Casual Writing** if you want a faster grammar check—but why bother checking stuff like that anyway?

Customize the Rules to Suit Yourself

If there are things that the grammar checker bugs you about and you wish it would quit, just turn them off. Scroll through the lists under either **Grammar** or **Style**, or both, and uncheck the boxes for things you don't want to be asked about. If you're not sure what a rule is about, click on **Explain** to see some examples.

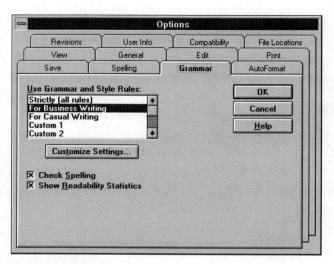

Figure 5.18 The Grammar tab

Set Maximum Number of Words per Sentence

If you're trying to write at a certain grade level, you can set the maximum number of words Word permits per sentence. If it finds a sentence longer than that, it will ask you to split that sentence into two. Normally, this is set at 35 words.

The AutoFormat Tab

Use the AutoFormat tab to customize how Word automatically formats a document. Normally, Word applies its autoformatting rules to all the elements that are checked in Figure 5.19. If there are things that you want Word to leave alone, uncheck those boxes. For example, if **Lists** is checked, Word deletes any paragraph numbers or bullets you've inserted manually and replaces them with its automatic paragraph numbers and bullets. Likewise, keeping **Tabs and Spaces** checked tells Word to remove two spaces between sentences automatically. Believe it or not, there are still some offices that insist on putting two spaces between sentences; even though you shouldn't do this when you are using a proportionally spaced typeface like Times or Arial. (Show this page to the person in your office who insists on two spaces between sentences. Every office has one.)

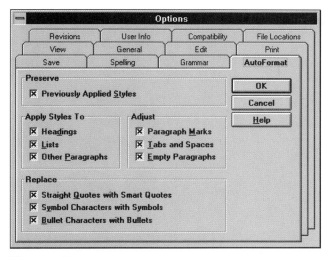

Figure 5.19 Word's autoformatting rules

What Next?

There are all sorts of other things you can change about the way Word behaves, and you'll see tricks for them throughout the book. In the next chapter, we'll look at tricks you can use with tables.

Chapter 6

· ·

Tables Tricks

As a general rule, if you have more than two or three entries that need to go into columns and rows, you'll be better off using a table. Tables are easy to set up and use, certainly if you use the slick tricks you'll find in this chapter.

If you're accustomed to figuring out where to set tab stops to set up a table—forget it. Use tabs only for a couple of columns, such as items with prices that require a decimal tab aligned dollars and cents. For everything else, use a real table.

Setting Up Tables

· ·

To create a table, just click the **Table** button on the **Standard** toolbar. Drag until the rows and columns are the size of the table you want (Figure 6.1); then release the mouse button and a new, empty table will appear (Figure 6.2).

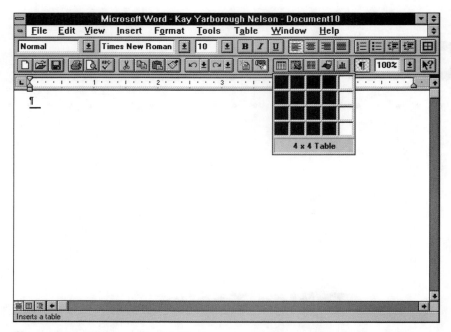

Figure 6.1   Click on the Table button and drag to create a table with the number of columns and rows you want.

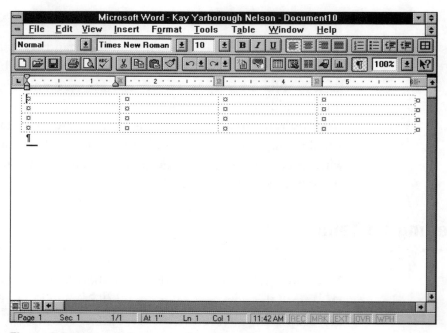

Figure 6.2   The table, ready for entering text

Use the Mouse to Set Up Tables

Most of the time, it's easier to set up and work with tables using the mouse. You can click on the **Table** icon on the toolbar and drag to set up the basic table structure, change column widths, select cells, rows, and columns, and so on. Use the keyboard for entering text in cells, but use the mouse to set up tables.

Use the Table Icon to Set Up a Big Table

The Table icon on the toolbar lets you set up a table as big as 16 rows and 10 columns. Although all you see is a 4 X 5 table when you click on the icon, just drag down or to the right to make the table grid bigger. Keep dragging until you've selected a table that's as many rows and columns as you want.

Yes, there's an Insert Table command on the Table menu (**Alt, a, i**) where you can specify how many rows you want, how many columns, the column width, and so on, but don't use it unless you're setting up a really big table.

Sizing Your Table

Don't know how big a table you want? Make a bigger one than you think you'll need. It's faster to delete leftover rows from tables than to add them as you need them in the middle of a table. So guess on the generous side when you're setting up a table and then just delete the part you don't use.

Set Up Your Table First

Although you can convert typed text to tables, if you haven't typed the text yet, it's much faster to set up the table structure and then enter the information in it. That way, you don't have to figure out where to set tab stops for the columns.

Shortcuts for Selecting in Tables

Use the mouse for selecting in tables. Here are a few mouse shortcuts for selecting in tables:

♦ Click at the beginning of the cell marker to select a cell's contents.

♦ Click on the left edge of the table to select the row.

♦ Double-click on a cell marker to select the row.

♦ Click on the top border of the table to select the column.

♦ Click and drag over cells, rows, and columns to select several of them at once.

♦ Shift-click to select several separate cells, rows, or columns.

In all these cases, the mouse cursor becomes an arrowhead when you click to select a cell, row, or column (see Figure 6.3).

There are Select Column and Select Row commands on the Table menu, but it's really faster to use the mouse than the menu.

The Mouse Cursor Changes Shape in Tables

There are three different shapes that the cursor can have when you're in a table. Each one relates to a different function:

♦ An I-beam cursor indicates that you can edit and type text.

♦ An arrow cursor indicates that you can click to select rows and columns.

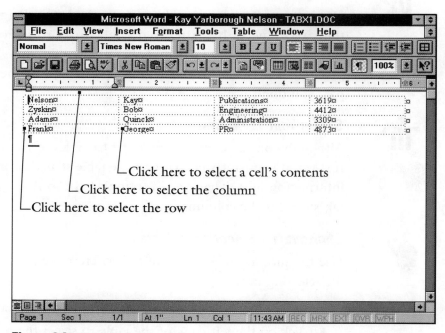

Figure 6.3 Selecting in tables

♦ A double-arrow cursor pointing to two straight lines means that you can drag a cell border to resize the table.

Select an Entire Table Instantly

To select the entire table, put the insertion point anywhere in the table and press **Alt+Num 5**. Instantly, the whole table is selected.

Gridlines Not Showing?

Choose gridlines from the Table menu (**Alt, a, l**) to turn on nonprinting gridlines. Gridlines make it easier to enter items in cells and to see what you have selected.

Slick Tricks for Inserting Columns and Rows

You'll love these hidden slick tricks. First, select a column or row:

♦ To select a row, click at the left of the table.
♦ To select a column, click at the top of the table.

Now click on the **Table** icon on the toolbar. You'll get a new row (or column, whichever you selected). The row will appear *above* the row you selected. The column will appear to the *left* of the column you selected.

Use the Table Shortcut Menu

Put the insertion point anywhere in a table and click with the right mouse button. You'll see the Table shortcut menu (Figure 6.4). It lets you insert rows, delete cells, change the font, and so on.

Inserting Cells in a Table

Here's the fastest way to add new cells to a table.

1 Select the same number of cells that you want to insert.
2 Click the **Insert Cell** button on the toolbar (it's the same as the Table button, but it takes on a new name when you're actually in a table).
3 You'll see the dialog box in Figure 6.5. Pick what you want to do.

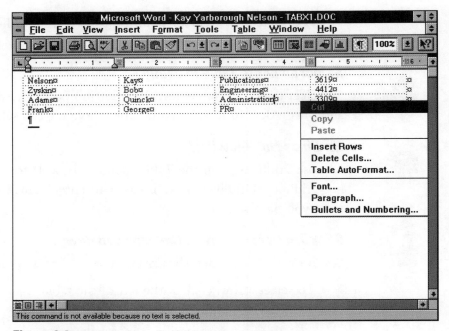

Figure 6.4 Displaying the Table shortcut menu

A Quick Method for Inserting a New Column or Row

Select the column to the left of where you want the new column to appear. Then click the Table button on the toolbar. The new column appears to the *left* of the column you selected.

To add a new row, select the row that you want the new row to appear next to; then click the Table button on the toolbar. The inserted row appears *above* the row you selected.

Inserting Rows at the Bottom of a Table

If you want to add a row to the bottom of the table, just go to the last cell in the last row (**Alt+End**, **Alt+PgDn**) and press **Tab**. If you're at the bottom of the table and you want to continue creating cells or entering information in them, just keep pressing **Tab** while you're there.

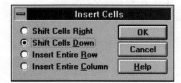

Figure 6.5 The Insert Cells dialog box

Another Method for Adding Rows

Word always creates a rectangular table. If you insert cells that add to the table's structure, the program will automatically fill in blank cells around them so that you don't have a few cells sticking out by themselves. Use this tip to create new rows: To insert extra columns and rows, highlight cells at the bottom of the table and choose **Shift Cells Down** from the Insert Cell button to create new rows at the same time.

Inserting a Column on the Right Side of a Table

If you want to insert the column on the far right of the table, it's just a little tricky, because Word wants to put new columns to the *left* of the current column. To get around this, you have to select the end-of-row markers first (see Figure 6.6). It's tricky to do this; the best way is to put the pointer above the markers and, when it turns into a downward-pointing arrow, click the mouse button.

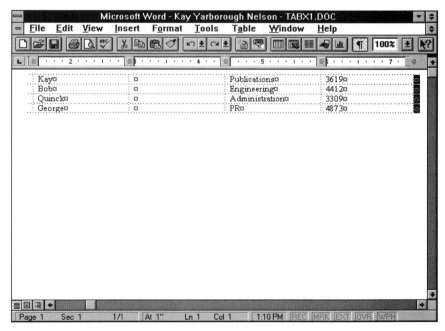

Figure 6.6   **Selecting the end of row markers**

Splitting a Table into Smaller Tables

Sometimes things get out of hand and you wind up with a huge table. For your readers' sake, consider splitting it into several small tables. Just put the insertion point between rows where you want the table to split and then press **Ctrl+Shift+Enter**. You'll get two smaller tables with a paragraph marker between them (see Figure 6.7).

Moving Around in Tables

. . . .

To move through a table, it's often easiest and simplest just to point and click with the mouse. You can also press the Right, Left, Down, and Up arrow keys to move through a table. And there are all sorts of other keyboard shortcuts you can use, as you'll see in the next tricks. The basic key to remember is the *Tab* key: Press **Tab** to move to the next cell clockwise, or **Shift+Tab** to move counterclockwise.

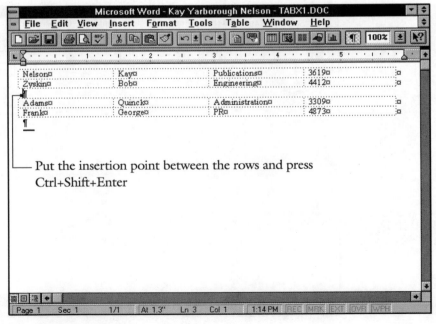

Figure 6.7   Splitting a table

Moving in Tables

There are all sorts of hard-to-memorize shortcuts about selecting cells in tables and moving through a table. Here are a few keyboard shortcuts that are easy to remember:

- **Home** and **End** move the insertion point to the beginning or end of the cell you're in.
- **Alt+Home** and **Alt+End** move the insertion point to the first or last cell in the row.
- **Alt+PgUp** and **Alt+PgDn** move the insertion point to the first or last cell in the column.
- **Tab** and **Shift+Tab** move to the next or previous cell and select its contents.
- **Ctrl+Left arrow** and **Ctrl+Right arrow** move to the next or previous cell without selecting its contents

You might also want to make a note of these combinations for moving to the first or last cell in a table. They're useful when you're working with a big table that you can't see completely on the screen.

- **Alt+PgUp**, **Alt+Home** to move to the first cell in a table.
- **Alt+PgDn**, **Alt+End** to move to the last cell in a table.

Tab Might Add a Row You Don't Want

If you press the Tab key when you're in the last cell of a table, you'll add a new row to the table. That may not be what you intend to do.

Deleting in Tables

Word lets you delete either a cell's contents or the cell (row or column) itself. If you're not careful, you can remove the structure of your table without intending to. So try a few of the tricks in this section to keep things simple.

Shortcuts for Deleting Table Contents

Naturally, Word has shortcuts for deleting the contents of cells, rows, and columns.

- ◆ To delete a cell's text, select it and press **Del**, or use **Ctrl+X**.

- ◆ To delete the contents of a row or column, select it and press **Del**, or use **Ctrl+X**.

- ◆ To delete all the contents of the table but leave its structure intact, select it (**Alt+Num 5**) and press Del.

To delete a cell, row, or column, click in the cell (if you're deleting just one cell) or select the cells, row(s), or column(s) to be deleted. Making sure the cursor stays within the selected area, click the right mouse button and choose **Delete**. Then from the **Delete Cells** menu, pick how you want the table to be rearranged. You can also use the **Delete** command on the **Table** menu, but the right mouse button is often faster.

Don't Use Backspace for Deleting Several Cells

Don't try to delete the contents of several cells with Backspace. If you try to delete with Backspace and you have several cells selected, you'll delete only the contents of the first cell. So use Del and Ctrl+X for deleting in tables.

Although you can use the Table menu's Delete commands or the Table's shortcut menu that you get when you press the right mouse button, the keyboard commands are usually faster.

Moving, Cutting, Copying, and Pasting in Tables

It takes a little patience to get used to all the techniques for moving and copying text and graphics from one cell to another, where the material appears when you copy or move it. Work with a few of these tricks, and you'll soon get the hang of it.

Copying and Cutting Rows and Columns

To copy a row or column, just select it and press **Ctrl+C**. To cut a row or column, select it using the **Select Row** or **Select Column** command in the **Table** menu. To paste the selected text, move to the place where you want it and press **Ctrl+V**. The other rows or columns shift *down* or to the *right* when you paste the copied or cut selection. (Note: Using Ctrl+X deletes only the contents of the row or column.)

Pasting Cut or Copied Cells

If you select any cells at the location where you're planning to paste cut or copied cells and they aren't exactly the shape of the cells you selected, you'll get a message saying that the paste failed. Instead, just put the insertion point at the upper-left corner of the cells you're replacing with the copied or cut cells and then paste. If the cells that are on the Clipboard need more rows in your table, Word will add rows to accommodate them.

Limitations of Cut and Copy in Tables

If you cut or copy a mixture of text and table, you won't be able to paste it into another table. If you select more than the contents of a table—such as surrounding text from the document—and cut or copy it, you won't be able to paste it into another table that you've created. You can only paste table material (rows and columns) into another table, or paste text material into another table cell.

Move Cells, Columns, and Rows by Dragging and Dropping Them

It's easy to edit a table. Just select a cell, column, or row (or several of them). Then release the mouse button, click in that area, and drag the selection to the new location where you want it in the table. Watch the cursor carefully; when you start to drag the selection, it changes to an arrowhead towing a small box. A dotted line will indicate the insertion point—where the selected cells will appear when you drop them. They'll appear to the *left* of that dotted line. This is another of those skills that takes getting used to.

If you find that you can't do drag-and-drop editing in tables, choose **Options** from the **Tools** menu, click the **Edit** tab, and make sure **Drag-and-Drop Text Editing** is checked.

Dragging and Copying

Press **Ctrl** as you drag if you're copying cells instead of moving them.

Changing Column Widths and Row Heights

In the past, editing tables was a time-consuming chore that could drive you blind. But using the tricks in this section—especially the ones that show you how to let Word do the walking instead of your fingers—can make editing tables much simpler and faster.

Adusting Column Widths

Let Word take care of adjusting column widths for you! Word has an AutoFit button in the Cell Height and Width dialog box. Go ahead and type your table without worrying about how it looks. Then select the table, choose **Cell Height and Width** from the **Table** menu, click the **Column** tab, and click **AutoFit**. Word will reformat your table and resize the columns according to what's in the table.

Automatically Resizing Columns

To have Word AutoFit all the columns in a table instead of resizing them column by column to fit the text that's there, just put the cursor on the far-left vertical grid line. When it changes to a double arrowhead, double-click the grid line. Word AutoFits all the column widths based on the text in the columns.

To have Word AutoFit just one column, double-click on the vertical grid line to the right of that column.

Although using AutoFit is faster, there will be times when you will need to resize tables yourself. Following are some tricks for resizing tables.

Using the Mouse to Change Column Widths

Tables start out with equal columns, but you'll often want to make a column a little bit wider or narrower. The easiest way to widen or narrow a column a little bit is simply to drag the column border with the mouse. The cursor will change to a double arrowhead. Your table will stay the same size; only the column width will change.

Changing the Width of Several Columns at Once

You can change column widths in several columns at the same time if you select them before you start dragging.

Controlling Other Changes

Remember, *something* has to give when you add or delete space in a table. Either column sizes will change or the table's overall size will change. Here are the secrets to controlling what changes:

♦ If you press **Shift** while you drag a column's border, only that column and the column to its immediate right will change.

♦ If you press **Ctrl** while you drag a column's border, all the column widths to the right of the column you're changing become equal.

♦ If you press **Ctrl+Shift** while you drag a column's border, you'll add width to the table, but the columns to the right of the column you're changing stay the same.

Remember that last one! Ctrl+Shift increases the table's size while keeping the columns the same size (except the one you're changing, of course).

Using the Ruler to Change Column Widths

You can also use the ruler to adjust columns in a table. Just drag the column markers on the ruler (Figure 6.8). The table's overall width won't change when you use the ruler this way.

Use the Table Menu for Exact Column Widths

If you don't want to "eyeball" column widths but instead want them exact to the nearest hundredth of an inch, use the **Cell Height and Width** dialog box. Select the first column you want to change, click the right mouse button while within the selected area, and you'll see the Columns shortcut menu (Figure 6.9). Choose **Cell Height and Width**. You'll see the column part of the Cell Height and Width dialog

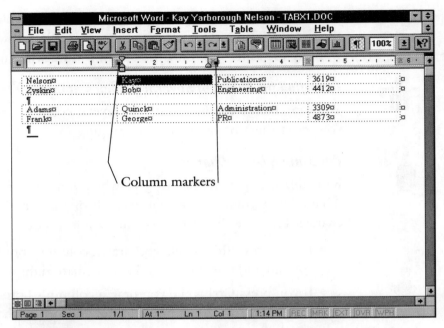

Figure 6.8 Drag column markers on the ruler to change column width.

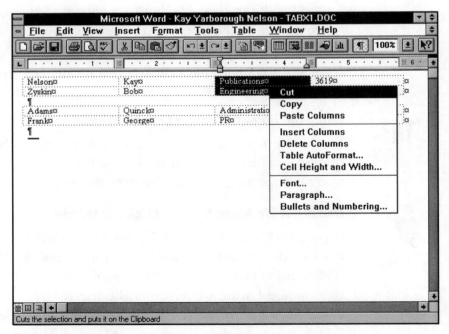

Figure 6.9 Using the Columns shortcut menu

box (Figure 6.10). Enter an exact width and click on **Next Column** to move to the next column until you've specified the exact widths you want for all the columns.

Changing Space between Columns

If you want to adjust the amount of white space between *all* the columns in a table, use the **Cell Height and Width** dialog box and enter a different measurement in the **Space Between Columns** box. The factory setting is .15". The overall size of the table won't change when you adjust the space between columns.

If you want more white space between two columns and less white space between two other columns, use this trick instead: Select each column and change its paragraph indent.

Changing Row Height

Normally, Word automatically adjusts the height of cells across the row to accept whatever text you type. If you want to specify an exact row height, triple-click the insertion point in the row, click the right mouse button, and choose **Cell Height and Width**. You'll see the row part of the Cell Height and Width dialog box shown in Figure 6.11.

Usually, you'll want to choose **At Least** from the pop-up list under **Height of Row** to put white space around cell entries, instead of specifying **Exactly**. If you choose Exactly and later need a taller row to accommodate a larger font or more text, the text in that row may get chopped off.

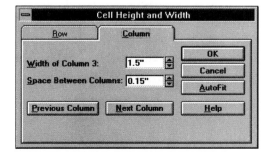

Figure 6.10 Changing column widths exactly in the Cell Height and Width dialog box

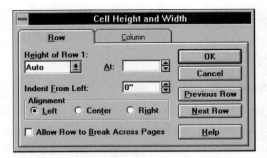

Figure 6.11   Changing row height

Changing Spacing between Rows

To change spacing between rows, use the Paragraph dialog box. Click in the table with the right mouse button and choose Paragraph; then click the Indents and Spacing tab. Enter measurements in the Before or After boxes.

Aligning a Narrow Table

To quickly center a table within the page margins: Select the table (**Alt+Num 5**) and choose **Cell Height and Width** from the **Table** menu (**Alt, a, w**); select the **Row** tab and choose **Center** under **Alignment**. You can also align a table flush right or flush left this way.

Forcing a Row to Stay on the Same Page

Word breaks a table within a row if the whole row doesn't fit on the page. Normally, this isn't a problem if there's only a little text in rows, but if you have several lines of text in the last row on a page, you may not want that row split between pages. To keep it from being split, uncheck the **Allow Row to Break Across Pages** box in the **Row** tab of the **Cell Height and Width** dialog box off the **Table** menu.

Making Big Cells out of Little Ones

I used to wonder how to make those nice banner headings that span several rows across a table, until I found this trick (see Figure 6.12): merge the whole row of cells into one big cell. You can also merge the cells in columns to make cells of varying sizes.

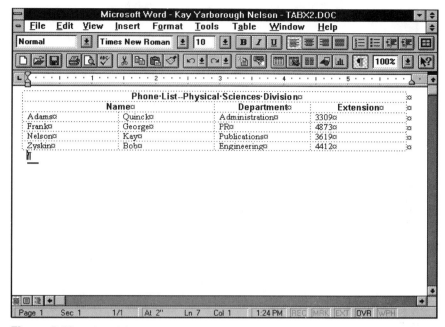

Figure 6.12 **A table using various sizes of cells**

Merging Cells

Here's the trick for creating those big cells: Select the rows or columns to be merged and choose **Merge Cells** from the **Table** menu (**Alt, a, m**). To create cells of various sizes, just select the cells and choose **Merge Cells**. Any text that was in those cells goes into the resulting cell, with paragraph markers (which you can delete) separating them.

Split Cells to Make Smaller Cells

Likewise, you can split larger cells into smaller ones. There's a Split Cells command on the Table menu (**Alt, a, p**). When you use it, Word suggests a number of columns to split the cells into, but you can type a different number.

When you split cells, if there's any text in the cell you split, the text winds up in the cell to the left and new, empty cells are created to the right. If there's more than one paragraph of text in the cell you're splitting, the paragraphs will appear in separate cells.

Repeating a Header Row on a New Page

If you have a table that takes up more than one page, you'll probably want to have the header row appear on subsequent pages of the table. It's easier to do this than you might think:

1 Select the row that you want to be repeated on each page.

2 Choose **Headings** from the **Table** menu (**Alt, a, h**).

3 To see how the table will look with the header row repeating across it, look at it in Page Layout view.

Header Rows Lost with Hard Page Breaks

One small trap: If you break the table with hard page breaks, that header row won't repeat. Word will repeat it only after soft page breaks (the kind that the program inserts automatically).

Formatting Tables

· ·

Once you've created a table, you can apply special formatting to it with the slick tricks in this section.

Putting Borders around Cells

It's easy to add borders and shading to tables for a very sophisticated touch. The easiest way is to use the Table AutoFormat feature.

1 With the insertion point anywhere in the table, click the right mouse button and choose **Table AutoFormat**. You'll see the dialog box shown in Figure 6.13.

2 Under **Formats**, choose a design that you like.

3 Pick the different formats you'd like to apply by selecting the check boxes under **Formats To Apply** and **Apply Special Formats To**.

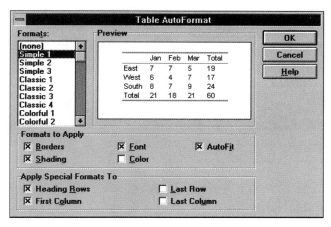

Figure 6.13 AutoFormatting a table

Adding Borders Using the Borders Button

For a quick way to add borders to a few cells in a table, click the **Borders** button on the **Standard** toolbar. The Borders toolbar appears. Just select the cells you want to have a border around, click on the buttons showing the different border styles on the Borders toolbar, and choose the one you want.

Add Shading to Cells for Visual Interest

Select the **Shading** drop-down list (Figure 6.14) from the end of the **Borders** toolbar, and use it to create fancy effects in your tables. You can use solid shading or a percentage. If you want text to be readable through the shading, choose 10 percent or, at the most, 15 percent.

Just select the cells and then pick the shading you want. Pick solid or a high percentage if you're using the shading for visual interest only—to divide sections of a table—with no text in the cells, for example.

Using the Borders and Shading Command

If you want a really sophisticated-looking table, try out some of the extra choices in the Borders and Shading dialog box (see Figure 6.15). To get to it, choose **Borders and Shading** from the **Format** menu (**Alt, o, b**); then click on the **Shading** tab. Under **Fill**, click on **Custom**; then, under **Shading**, scroll to the end of the list to view the pattern choices.

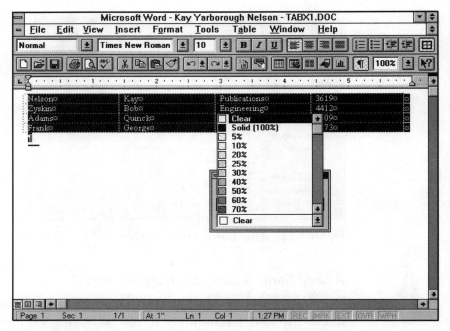

Figure 6.14   The shading drop-down list on the Borders toolbar

To apply shading and patterns to cells with this dialog box, select the cells and pick the effect you want. Watch the Preview box to see how it will look. Click OK to apply the effect to your table.

Avoid Patterns with Text

   Don't use a pattern if there's text in the cells you are shading, or you won't be able to read the text.

Formatting Text in Cells

You can format characters in cells just as in any other part of a Word document. Press **Ctrl+B** for boldface, **Ctrl+I** for italics, and so forth.

Each cell's text is considered a paragraph, so you can use the same tricks you saw back in Chapter 3 to align text:

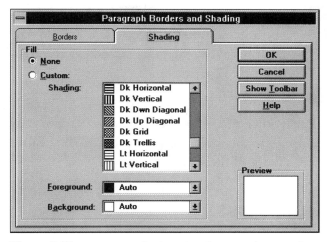

Figure 6.15 Pattern choices in the Borders and
Shading dialog box

Ctrl+R	Right align
Ctrl+E	Center
Ctrl+J	Justify
Ctrl+M	Indent
Ctrl+T	Hanging indent
Ctrl+Q	Remove paragraph formats

Review Chapter 3 for more text formatting shortcuts.

Inserting a Tab in a Table

Normally when you're in a table, pressing Tab moves to and selects the
next cell. If you want to insert a tab in a table cell, use **Ctrl+Tab**.

Save Your Table's Structure to Use It Again

The process of formatting a table with fancy borders, centered headings,
and so on, can be time-consuming. If you create a table you like, save it
as an AutoText entry so that you can use that same structure again.

To save it as an AutoText entry:

 Select the first few rows of the table. You don't have to select
the whole table, because all you want to save is its structure.
Your new tables will have different contents but will be based
on this structure.

2 Choose **AutoText** from the **Edit** menu (**Alt, e, x**).

3 Type a name for the table. Use a unique name that helps you remember what the table is, such as **monthlyreport** (you can use up to 32 characters).

4 Click on **Add**.

When you're ready to use that table structure again, just type the name you gave the table and click the AutoText button on the Standard toolbar. That's all there is to it.

Miscellaneous Table Tricks

In this section are all sorts of tables tricks that couldn't be classified as anything but "miscellaneous." You may find exactly what you need here.

Converting Text to Tables

If your table text has already been typed and aligned with tabs, you can easily convert it to a table without having to type it again. Just select the text and then click the **Table** button on the toolbar. You'll probably need to go back and adjust the width of the columns.

If you need to control exactly how Word divides the text into columns and rows, use the **Convert Text To Table** command on the **Table** menu. But most of the time, just selecting the text and clicking the Table button will be all you need to do.

Converting a Table to Text

It works both ways: You can also convert tables to regular text. There's no slick shortcut for it, though; you'll have to use a menu.

First, select the table that you want to convert to text. Then choose **Convert Table to Text** from the **Table** menu. You'll see a dialog box similar to the one shown in Figure 6.16, asking how you want the columns separated—with tabs, paragraph marks, or commas. Tabs is the default.

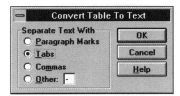

Figure 6.16 Converting a table to text

Quickly Alphabetizing a Table

Suppose you have a table of names and addresses (like the one shown in Figure 6.17) that you'd like to get in alphabetical order. Or you may have a neatly alphabetized table that you want to add more entries to. Instead of painstakingly dragging or inserting rows to get them in alphabetical order, just sort the rows in the table.

1 Select the rows you want to sort.

2 Choose **Sort** from the **Table** menu (**Alt, a, t**). You'll see the dialog box shown in Figure 6.18.

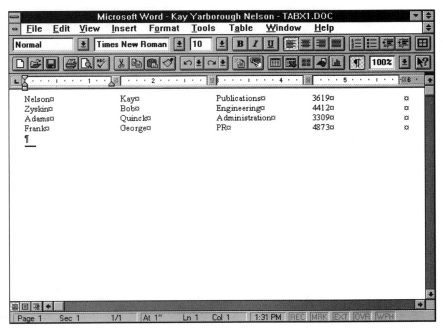

Figure 6.17 The table before sorting it

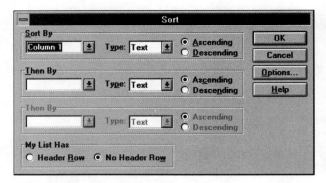

Figure 6.18 The Sort dialog box

3 Under **Sort By**, use the first column (you can select any column you want to use as the sort order, but in Figure 6.19, the first column is sorted by last name).

4 Choose **Text** under **Type**, and click on **Ascending**.

5 Click OK. Your table will be sorted based on that column (see Figure 6.19).

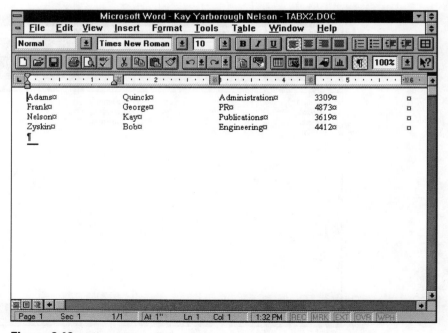

Figure 6.19 The table after sorting it

You can do this with numerical lists, too, to sort phone numbers by area code or mailing lists by zip code.

Calculating Numbers

Adding up totals of numbers in a column or row of a table is easier and quicker than you may think. Just put the insertion point in the cell where you want the total to appear, such as the last cell in a column or row. Then choose **Formula** (**Alt, a, o**) from the **Table** menu and click OK in the Formula dialog box.

If Word can't figure out what kind of calculation you're trying to make, you'll see an = in the Formula dialog box. If you see this, click the Help button to get help on what you're trying to do. Word usually assumes you're trying to add (sum) the numbers in the cells.

What Next?

Printing, of course. Try as we might, it's not a paperless world yet.

Chapter 7

· ·

Printing

Printing is an area where we could all use some slick tricks. Space limitations won't let me give tips for specific printers, so this chapter's full of tricks you can use with just about any printer.

Installing Your Printer

The important thing to remember before you start printing in Word is that you have to install your printer through Windows. If you don't have a printer installed yet, go to the **Windows Control Panel** and double-click on the **Printer** icon.

Once you've done that, you can choose **Print** from the **File** menu, click on the **Printer** button, and select the printer you've just installed. Click on the **Set as Default Printer** button in the **Print Setup** dialog box if you want to use that printer most of the time.

Quick Printing

Click on the **Print** icon in the **Standard** toolbar to quickly print one complete copy of the document you're working on. Pressing **Ctrl+P** or

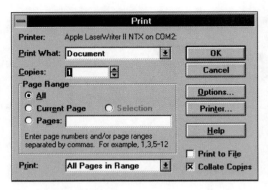

Figure 7.1 Options in the Print dialog box

Ctrl+Shift+F12 takes you to the Print dialog box (Figure 7.1), where you can choose which pages you want to print, how many copies, and so forth.

Printing the Current Page

To print just the page where the insertion point is, choose **Print** from the File menu (or press **Ctrl+Shift+F12**) and click **Current Page** and **OK**.

   Ctrl+Shift+F12, **Alt+E**, **Enter** is a quick keyboard shortcut for this. You might want to make it into a macro and assign it to an icon if you find that you're printing the current page often.

Printing Selected Pages

You can simply enter the page numbers you want to print in the Print dialog box if you don't want to print the whole document or the current page. To print just one page, press **Ctrl+P** and enter the page number in the **Pages** box.

   If there are sections in your document, you can use a little cryptic shorthand to tell Word which pages you want printed. Use S for the section number and P for the page number. For example, to print from Section 1, page 5 to Section 3, page 4, press **Ctrl+P**, then enter p5s1-p4s3.

Printing Only Even or Odd Pages

If you want to print only the even or odd pages of a document, choose **Odd Pages** or **Even Pages** from the list under **Print** in the **Print** dialog box.

You can combine this trick with printing a range of pages. For example, if you want just the odd pages from page 50 to page 100 printed out, type the page range as 50-100 and choose **Odd Pages** in the **Print** dialog box.

Print to Suit Yourself

You can set print options in Word that will apply to all the documents you print. Unfortunately, everything can't be completely automated: You'll still need to tell Word how many copies you want and whether you want to print the entire document or just part of it. But you can set other options, such as always printing in draft quality or printing document summary information at the end of each document.

To use the Print options, choose **Options** from the **Tools** menu (**Alt, t, o**) and click on the **Print** tab (Figure 7.2).

Avoid Printing Graphics
For fast hard copy of your text only, check the **Draft Output** check box. Graphics won't be printed when this box is checked.

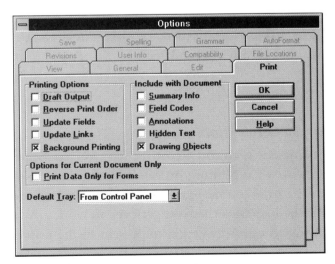

Figure 7.2 Setting print options

No Draft Output with Laser Printers

Checking Draft Output won't do you any good if you have a laser printer. Laser printers print only in high quality anyway, so you won't save any time by checking the Draft Output box. If you have a dot-matrix printer, though, checking this box speeds up printing, because Word uses the printer's default draft font and doesn't apply any character or frame formatting.

Reverse Print Order

Some printers print in reverse numeric order so that the last page comes out on top and you have to restack them all. If your printer does this, click on **Reverse Print Order**, and page one will come out on top. (It will slow down printing speed, though.)

The Update Fields Box

Uncheck the **Update Fields** box in the **Print Options** dialog box if you don't want to update fields when you print. If Update Fields is checked, Word updates the fields when it prints your document. If this isn't what you intend—for example, if you have a date field that should remain as that particular date—uncheck the Update Fields box so that it won't be updated.

Work While You Print

Checking **Background Printing** lets you continue working on your document while printing proceeds in the background. You'll find that the entire print job may take longer with this box checked than without it, but the benefit is that you get back to work in Word quicker, instead of having to wait for the job to be sent to the printer.

Printing Annotations and Hidden Text

If you are using Word's annotation and hidden text features for incorporating comments from a workgroup into a document, check **Annotations** or **Hidden Text**, or both, to get a printed copy of the comments.

Printing on Another Printer

Here's a slick trick called *printing to a file*. It lets you print a document without using Word—even using a computer that doesn't have Word installed on it. This is a neat way to set up a document to print on a printer that isn't connected to your computer. Not all printers can do this as easily as PostScript printers can.

1. Install the printer you ultimately plan to print the document on (see the sidebar "Installing Windows Printers" at the end of this chapter). That printer doesn't have to be connected to your computer, or even in the same building! Just install it so that Word can format a document for it.

2. Choose **Print** from the **File** menu or press **Ctrl+P**.

3. Choose the **Printer** button and select the printer you're planning to print the document on.

4. Click on **Set As Default Printer** and **Close**.

5. Check the **Print To File** box and click on **OK**.

6. In the **Output File Name** box, type a name for the file. Don't use the file's original name! Try to include something that helps you remember which printer the document is prepared for, such as "Hpchap1.prn." Include a path to your floppy disk drive, because you'll undoubtedly be taking the file with you on a floppy disk.

See the next trick for how to print it out if Word isn't handy.

Printing on Just About Any Printer

If you're not sure which printer's going to be available, you can use this slightly more complex slick trick to set up a file so that you can print it on any printer, even if the computer that's controlling that printer isn't running Windows. You print from DOS.

1 Go to the **Print Manager** and choose **Printer Setup** from the **Options** menu.

2 Pick the printer you want to print the file to—it doesn't have to be attached to your computer, but it does have to be installed.

3 Click on **Connect** and choose **FILE** as the port to connect to (Figure 7.3).

4 Click on **OK** and close the dialog box. Exit from Print Manager.

5 Then go back to Word and choose **Print** to print the current document to that file. You'll be asked to fill out the **Print To File** dialog box with the file name you want to use. You may want to include a hint about which printer it's formatted for in the file's name, such as DJLTTR for a letter prepared for a H-P DeskJet.

Now, with that file on a floppy disk, you can take it to any computer that's running DOS and the printer you formatted the file for. To print it when you're at the other computer, use the PRINT command at the DOS prompt. For example, to print a document called MEMO.TXT that's on a floppy disk in drive A using a printer attached to the first parallel port on that computer, you'd enter **print a:memo.txt** at the DOS prompt and press **Enter**.

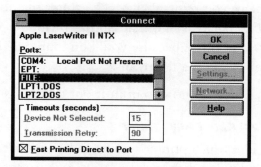

Figure 7.3 Connect to FILE instead of a port in the Windows Connect dialog box so that you can print to disk.

If the printer doesn't print, try putting LPT2, LPT3, COM1, COM2, or COM3 after REPORT.TXT until you figure out which port the printer's attached to. Or check the back of your computer if you know which port is what.

Using the COPY Command

Can't print the whole document with the PRINT command? Try the COPY command instead. If the PRINT command doesn't print the whole document, there may be a Ctrl+Z somewhere in your document. When DOS encounters a Ctrl+Z, it assumes that this marks the end of the file and stops printing. To fix that problem, use the COPY command instead (DOS will print with either command). Do it like this: Use the /B switch to force it to copy the whole file based on its size, not on any stray Ctrl+Zs that could be hiding in the file:

```
copy memo.txt /b lpt1
```

Printing from Find File

If you've used **Find File** to locate the document you want to print, just click on the **Commands** button after the file you want has been located (Figure 7.4). Then choose **Print**. Don't bother opening the document and then using the Print command.

Ctrl-click to select several files and then click Print to send them to the printer.

Save a Document after You Print It

If you want page breaks in your document on disk to exactly match those in your printed document, make it a habit to save each document immediately after you print it. That way, you'll know that the pagination in the document on disk is the same as in the printed document.

Save a Tree: Use Print Preview

If you make it a habit to use Print Preview (Figure 7.5) before printing a document, you'll save yourself a lot of paper. Print preview lets you

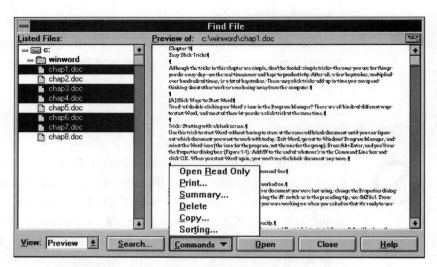

Figure 7.4 Choose Print to print selected files

see things you can't see in Normal view, such as precise alignment. Remember, there's a Print Preview button on the Standard toolbar. It's the page with the magnifying glass.

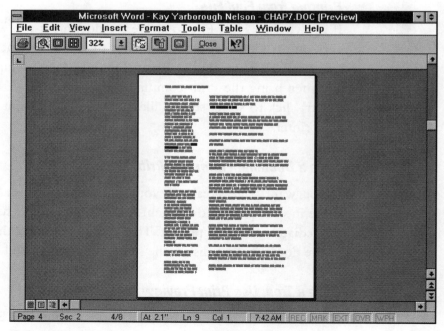

Figure 7.5 Viewing a page in Print Preview

Make Changes While in Print Preview

You can edit the text in Print Preview as well as reformat columns and change the page layout. The **Page Setup** command on the **File** menu and the **Columns** command on the **Format** menu are available to you, or you can use the mouse, as you'll see in the next tricks.

Can't Edit in Print Preview?

If you can't figure out how to edit text in Print Preview because you're toggling back and forth between Zoom In and Zoom Out as you click, use this tip: Click on the magnifier button on the toolbar again (the one with the magnifying glass) when the text is large enough to read easily. Now you'll be able to edit it.

Back to Normal View

To return to normal view from Print Preview quickly, click on the **Normal** button on the horizontal scroll bar.

Moving Around in Print Preview

You can click with the mouse to move from area to area in Print Preview, or you can use the keyboard shortcuts **Ctrl+Up arrow** and **Ctrl+Down arrow**. Sometimes a keyboard shortcut is faster than reaching for the mouse.

Reformatting in Print Preview

Use the mouse to change margins, column widths, and other page elements while in Print Preview. Just display the ruler and then drag a header, footer, frame, margin marker, column marker, or frame border marker to adjust its placement in Print Preview.

Seeing Measurements

Press the **Alt** key as you drag a marker while in Print Preview. You'll see exact measurements displayed on the ruler.

If you want control over how far the margins are from the edges of the paper, watch the number on the ruler as you drag the margin marker. It shows you the distance to the edge of the paper.

Be Careful When Changing Margins in Print Preview

You may think you're changing margins just on the page you're looking at, but you're not. Margin changes you make in Print Preview affect the whole document, even the pages that occur before the page you're on.

If you're using sections, however, only the pages that are in the current section will have their margins changed.

More Control over Margins

You can also change margins by choosing **Page Setup** from the **File** menu (**Alt, f, u**). That's what you should do if you need to set margins precisely (in hundredths of an inch) or if you want margin changes to affect the document only from the page where you are to the end of the document (under **Apply To**, choose **This Point Forward**). So if you want to change margins on only one page, use **Page Setup**, set the margins you want, move to the next page, and change them back to what they were. Chapter 4 has more page formatting tricks.

Zooming In and Out in Print Preview

Just click on the text area to switch back and forth from looking at a full-page view in Print Preview to look at an enlarged view. Click again to return to the view you were looking at before you clicked.

Moving through Pages in Print Preview

Press **PgDn** and **PgUp** to move through your document in Print Preview. Or click on the **Multiple Pages** button and drag to choose the number of pages you want to have displayed at once; then zoom in on the page you want to view.

Print from Print Preview

After you've reviewed the document, if you like what you see, just print it. That's what the Print button is there for. You can print just the pages you specify, too, as you saw in the tricks for the Print dialog box at the beginning of this chapter.

Miscellaneous Printing Tricks

Need a printing trick or two for envelopes and labels? Check out what's in this section.

Printing an Envelope

Let Word print envelopes for you. Don't fool with setting up their format from scratch. Use the **Envelopes and Labels** command on the **Tools** menu (**Alt, t, e**).

If you've already typed an address in your document, select the address. Then choose **Envelopes and Labels** and click on the **Envelope** tab (Figure 7.6). If you don't select an address first, Word looks for what it thinks may be an address, which may or may not be the text you want. Usually it's pretty accurate, but selecting the delivery address yourself is a sure-fire way to get the right address on the envelope.

You can also type the address directly into the dialog box if you haven't typed the address into the letter yet.

If your return address isn't correct, edit it. Word automatically takes the return address from the information stored in the User Info tab in the Options dialog box (choose **Options** from the **Tools** menu and click on the **User Info** tab). If your return address isn't coming up correctly, change it here.

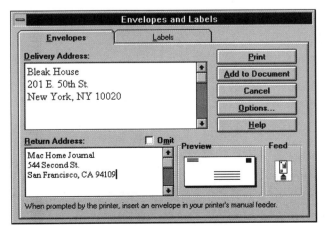

Figure 7.6 **Addressing an envelope**

You can print the envelope now or click on **Add To Document** so that the envelope will be added as a section at the beginning of the document. That way, it will be stored with the letter if you ever need to print the letter again or modify it for a new use.

Printing Just the Envelope

If you've stored an envelope as part of a document and want to print just the envelope, print page 0. That's where the envelope is stored.

Printing a Bar Code

Printing a bar code on envelopes can help speed up their delivery by the U.S. Post Office. If your printer can print graphics, you can have Word print a bar code on an envelope, along with the address. From the **Tools** menu, select **Envelopes and Labels**, click on the **Options** button on the **Envelopes** tab, and you'll see the options you can use (Figure 7.7).

Printing a Logo on an Envelope

If your company logo is stored as a graphic that Word can print, you can add it to your return address. Just fill out the **Envelopes** tab as you saw in the preceding tricks, with the correct return and delivery addresses. Then switch to page layout view and insert the graphic by choosing **Picture** from the **Insert** menu. You can position the graphic where you want it by dragging it.

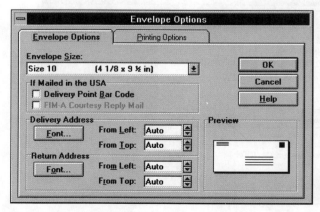

Figure 7.7 Setting envelope options

To have Word automatically insert your graphic as the return address on envelopes, select the graphic image. Then choose **AutoText** from the **Edit** menu (**Alt, e, x**). In the **Name** box, type EnvelopeExtra1 and click on **Add**.

Printing Mailing Labels

If you're not doing mail merge (and most of us aren't), you may find it a little difficult to figure out how to print just plain old mailing labels. You face the problem of having a big sheet of laser labels, but only one address you want to create mailing labels for. Word can print a single label or a whole sheet full of them going to the same address.

If you're going to be sending several things to one address over a period of time, print out a whole sheet of labels for that address and store it somewhere handy. That's what I do. Then I just grab a label and stick it on a package or big envelope when I need one. Either way, whether you're printing just one label at a time or a whole sheet of them, use this procedure:

1 Choose **Envelopes and Labels** from the **Tools** menu; click on the **Labels** tab. You'll see the dialog box shown in Figure 7.8.

2 Fill out the delivery address.

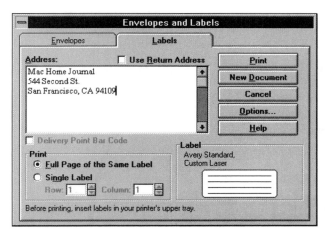

Figure 7.8 The Labels tab

3 Click on the **Options** button, or click on the sample mailing label in the lower right corner of the dialog box.

4 From the **Label Options** dialog box that you'll see (Figure 7.9), choose the type of labels you're using. (Look at the box they came in.) Then choose **OK**.

5 Choose either **Single Label** or **Full Page of the Same Label**. If you're printing a single label, type the row and column number of the label you want to print (look at the sheet of labels).

6 Put a sheet of labels in your printer and click on the **Print** button on the **Standard** toolbar or press **Ctrl+P**.

It's a good idea to test-print on a blank sheet of paper first. Then hold the real laser label sheet up to the light along with the printed sheet and make sure the labels are printing in the correct area(s). That way, you won't waste an expensive sheet of labels. If your labels aren't printing correctly, choose **Options** and then click on the **Details** button. You'll be able to specify exact measurements in the dialog box that you'll see (Figure 7.10)

Getting Specific Printer Help

The Print Setup dialog box you get depends on the printer you've installed and selected. Each printer has a different set of options. To get help on what they are, be sure to use the **Help** button in the **Print Setup** dialog box. If you press **F1**, you'll just get general printing help.

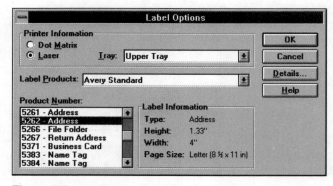

Figure 7.9   The Label Options dialog box

Troubleshooting Printing

If your printing isn't going right, try to isolate the source of the problem. First, check to see that the printer is on and the cable connections are tight. Then go to the Print Manager and see if there are any messages about what may be going wrong. Delete all your print jobs except the one that's indicated as currently printing. Check that your print options are correct and that the printer that's selected is the one you're trying to print with.

Go to the Control Panel, click on the Printer icon, and see if the Print Manager has been turned off. Turn it on if it's off and try printing again. Or if it's on, turn it off and see if the document will print now.

Try printing from Write or Notepad, and if you can print from there, the problem is probably in the program you're trying to print from, not in Windows. Check the Printer Setup dialog box in your program and make sure you are using the right printer.

As a last resort, try printing from DOS. If you have a non-PostScript printer connected to LPT1, type this at the DOS prompt:

    copy con lpt1
    testing

Then press **F6** (or **Ctrl**+z) and **Enter**.

If you have a Postscript printer, try a different tactic. There's a TESTPS.TXT file that comes with Windows and is stored in your C:\WINDOWS\SYSTEM directory. Test-print it like this at the DOS prompt:

    copy c:\windows\system\testps.txt com1

If you can print from DOS but can't print from Windows, the problem could be that there's not enough memory for the temporary print files. You need at least 2 Mb of free space in whatever directory is supposed to hold temporary files. Check your AUTOEXEC.BAT and see which directory that is; it'll be the one specified after TEMP=.

One last thing you can try before calling Microsoft (or your program's manufacturer if you've determined that the problem is coming from there) is to try printing to LPT1.DOS, LPT2.DOS, or LPT1.OS2[1] instead of to LPT1. Use the Printers icon in the Control Panel and connect to LPT2.DOS; then try printing from there. This little trick forces Windows to think you're printing to a file, not a printer port, but it sends the document to LPT1 anyway.

If you don't see these "ports" (they're actually DOS device names) listed, you'll need to add them to your list of ports. To do that, first make a copy of your WIN.INI file; then edit WIN.INI (just enter win.ini in the Program Manager's Run box and press Enter). Locate the [ports] section and add the lines:

LPT1.DOS=

LPT2.DOS=

Save WIN.INI and exit the Notepad; then restart Windows. You should be able to use the Printers Control Panel and click the Connect button to see the DOS "ports" now.

[1] If you upgraded from Windows 3.0, you may see LPT1.OS2 in the Connect dialog box.

There's lots more printer help stored in Windows. If you have a Post-Script printer, read the file PRINTERS.WRI in your Windows directory for lots more PostScript printer tips, such as how to change the timeout if you're getting timeout messages, how to get mirror images and

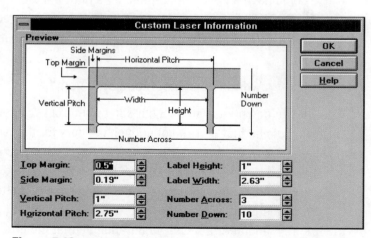

Figure 7.10 Specifying exact measurements for labels

Installing Windows Printers

Here's the quick course in installing printers. First, find your Windows Setup disks, because you're going to need one of them. Then double-click on the **Printers** icon in the **Control Panel**. You'll see a list of the Windows printers you've installed. Click **Add Printer** and select your printer from the list (just type the first letter of its name to go to that part of the alphabet). When your printer's name is highlighted, click **Install**. You'll be asked to insert the appropriate Windows Setup disk that has the printer driver on it. Then click **Configure** and tell Windows which port your printer is connected to, if it isn't on LPT1. As the last step, click **Setup** and see if there are any options you need to change.

You can install more than one printer, even if they're not all really attached to your computer. If you have one kind of printer at work and another at home, install both on both machines. Then you can format documents that are going to be printed on either one just by selecting that printer when you work on the document.

You may also want to install several printers when you're going to be traveling with a laptop. If you're going to be traveling with your laptop and printing from whatever printer happens to be available, install all the printers you think you might come across. Including a HP LaserJet is a pretty safe bet, and you might want to add an Epson dot-matrix printer and a PostScript printer, too.

reversed-out (negative images), how to reduce and enlarge documents, and so forth. There are too many of them to describe here, and if you don't have a PostScript printer, you probably don't want to read about them.

Even if you don't have a PostScript printer, read PRINTERS.WRI. There are tips in it for all different kinds of printers and programs. For instance: Printing Word for Windows envelopes on a HP DeskJet 500, printing Windows 3.0 documents on a HP LaserJet III . . . find out for yourself.

Read the file NETWORKS.WRI for details about printing via specific networks, setting up passwords, viewing the files in the network's queue, and so on. What you can do depends on the network you're using.

Printer Setup Affects All of Your Windows Programs

The Printer Setup dialog box that you get in Word (by choosing **Print** from the **File** menu, then clicking on the **Printer** button) is exactly the same as the one you get in Windows when you double-click on the **Printers** icon in the **Control Panel**. If you change settings in it, you change them for all your other Windows programs. Use the Page Setup command on the Format menu to change things like paper size, switch from Portrait to Landscape orientation, and so forth. Don't use Print Setup unless you really are changing settings that you want to be in effect in all your programs.

What Next?

• •

Now that we've covered a lot of printing tricks, we've run out of logical categories. The next chapter will cover all sorts of tricks for all sorts of subjects.

Chapter 8

All Sorts of Slick Tricks

THE TRICKS IN THIS CHAPTER fall into quite a few categories: using *fields* (you can really do some neat stuff with this feature), using the drawing tools, working with *templates* and *styles*, using Word's built-in macros to do things you probably thought you couldn't do . . . Quite frankly, this chapter has everything that wouldn't logically fit anywhere else.

Tricks with Fields

Word has a feature called *fields* that you may have been using all along without even knowing you were doing it. A field in Word is a buried set of instructions that tells the program to go and do something—get the date or the current page number, or even look in another document and use text from it. Using the fields feature isn't "hard": In fact, you can do some great tricks with it without knowing much at all.

Playing Fields

Word has a huge assortment of fields, and quite a few of them are used for sophisticated things, like automating mail merges and so forth. We won't get into those, but here's a list of the most useful of Word's fields and what they can automate in your documents:

Author	Inserts the author of the document (from the Summary Information box).
Date	Inserts the current date.
CreateDate	Inserts the date the document was created.
EditTime	Inserts the number of minutes spent working on the document.
FileName	Inserts the file name of the document.
NumChars	Inserts the number of characters in the document.
NumPages	Inserts the number of pages in the document (useful for headers like "Page 3 of 52").
NumWords	Inserts the number of words in the document.
Page	Inserts the current page number.
SaveDate	Inserts the date the document was last saved.
Subject	Inserts the subject from the Summary Information box.
Time	Inserts the current time.
Title	Inserts the document's title (from the Summary Information box).
UserAddress	Inserts the return address used when you used the Envelope macro.
UserInitials	Inserts your initials.
UserName	Inserts the name you provided when you installed Word.

When you insert a field, it appears shaded in your document. Don't worry; the shading won't print. It's there to let you know that this is an automatic result and not something you typed in by hand.

Inserting Fields

To insert a field, choose **Field** from the **Insert** menu (**Alt, i, e**) and then pick the field you want to insert from the Field dialog box (see Figure 8.1). Remember, just as in most lists you can choose from in a dialog box, just type the first character of the field's name to go straight to that part of the list.

Inserting the Date and Time

Although you can insert the date and time from the Fields dialog box, there's a separate Date and Time command on the Insert menu that makes inserting these a little faster. To insert the date or the time (or both), press **Alt, i, t** and then click on the **Options** button and choose the format you want to use. Or use these handy keyboard shortcuts:

> **Alt+Shift+D** inserts the current date.
>
> **Alt+Shift+T** inserts the current time.
>
> The current date or time appears in your document.

Keep the Same Date by Locking the Field

If you don't want the current date put in your date fields when you print the document, or if you don't want the time to change, lock the field.

To lock a field, put the insertion point in it and press **Ctrl+F11**. To unlock it, use **Ctrl+Shift+F11**.

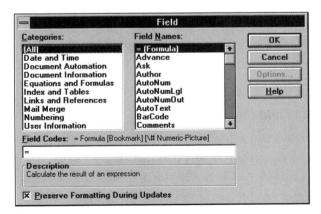

Figure 8.1 Inserting a field

Locking a field just prevents Word from updating it. If you know you'll never want to update a field, you can convert it to text. Just put the insertion point anywhere in the field, and press **Ctrl+Shift+F9**. This converts the date or time, or whatever's in the field, into text. It isn't an easy combination to remember, and you probably won't use it much, but it's not on any menu, so remember that you read about it here.

Displaying the Date When You Start

This is a neat trick for seeing the current date when you open a document. Go to the beginning of your document (**Ctrl+Home**) and choose **Field** from the **Insert** menu; then click under **Field Names** and select **Date**. (If you type **d**, you'll select Database; be careful). Then choose the **Options** button and pick the format you want the date to be displayed in. Double-clicking on **MMMM d, yyyy**, for example, gives you the date like this: January 14, 1994.

Deleting a Field

Sometimes you'll try to delete a field, but Word just beeps at you. The trick is to drag over the field to select it. Now press **Del** or **Backspace** to delete it.

Inserting the Current Page Number

The shortcut **Alt+Shift+P** inserts the current page number at the insertion point. This is a neat shortcut for getting the page number into a document's text. What it really does is insert a field, which you'll see if you try to delete it. Word beeps at you unless you select the page number before you try to delete it.

Viewing Field Codes

To see what the actual field codes look like, put the insertion point anywhere in the result and press **Shift+F9**. Press **F9** to view the result again. Usually you'll never need to see the codes unless you're doing fairly sophisticated programming in Word.

Type the Codes Instead of Inserting Them

If you know the special code, you can just type it in your document without using any menus or dialog boxes. Just press **Ctrl+F9**, and two curly braces appear in your document. Type the real name of the code. For example, to insert a date field, press **Ctrl+F9**, type **date,** and press **F9** to see the results (see the next trick).

To check on what a code is and how to use it, use the **Fields** dialog box (**Alt, i, e**). Highlight the field name and then look at what's showing in **Field Codes** (see Figure 8.2). Just above it, you'll see its syntax, or an example of how to use it. Here, for example, you can type in a prompt that the users will see on the screen, such as "Enter recipient's address."

Updating Fields

Just as in life, the information in a field isn't always accurate. Suppose you've inserted the current time, for example, but that was several hours ago; you want your document to show the current time *now*. Just put the insertion point anywhere in the field and press **F9**.

Word automatically updates date, page number, and time fields when you print a document.

Updating All the Fields in a Document

If you have several different fields in a document—for example, a date and time field, or several calculated fields—you can update them all at

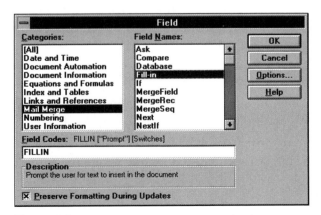

Figure 8.2 Finding out what a code does

once with this trick. First, select the entire document by pressing **Ctrl+A** or Ctrl-clicking in the selection bar to the left of the document. Then press **F9**.

Moving to the Next Field

If you're going through a document checking fields to make sure they're right, use this shortcut: **F11** takes you to the next field; **Shift+F11** takes you to the previous field.

Getting a Word Count

Getting a word count can be useful if you're writing magazine articles or doing word processing and are paid by the word. Word maintains information about your document, such as the number of words it contains, how many times it's been revised, how much time has been spent on it, and so on. To get a word count, choose **Word Count** from the **Tools** menu (**Alt**, **t**, **w**).

Inserting a Word Count in a Document

Checking on your word count in the Summary Information box won't automatically print the word count anywhere in your document, however. If you need a printed word count, put a NumWords field in your document.

Go to the place in your document where you want the word count to appear—after your byline, for example, at the end of the document, or in a header or footer. Type Word Count: (so that folks will know what that number is for) and press **Ctrl+F9**. Type numwords (this is the shortcut method) and press **F9** to see the result.

Update Your Word Count

If you are working on a document, the word count won't be accurate until you update. Put the insertion point in the field and press **F9** for an accurate word count. The word count will be automatically updated when you print the document, but the number on the screen won't be accurate if you keep on editing—cutting and adding new words.

Tricks with Templates, Wizards, and Styles

Save yourself even more time in Word by using its built-in templates and Wizards. Word comes with a lot of standard documents that are already formatted for you. Wizards, which are templates that prompt you for information by using dialog boxes, can really automate the process of creating documents. You can use these templates as is, modify them to suit yourself, or even set up your own templates for documents you use all the time. Then just let your fingers do the walking.

Templates also have *styles* in them. Styles are just paragraph and character formats that have been given names so that you can use the same format repeatedly. Once a style has been created, you simply apply it to a paragraph or some selected text, without having to go through all the steps needed to create that format again. To change the format, all you have to do is apply a different style. Styles make formatting much, much easier, and they also make sure that your formatting is consistent. No more wondering exactly which font you used, which margin settings, and so on. Just apply the style and let Word remember all of that for you, and your documents will always end up the way they started out. If you've ever changed tabs or switched fonts in the middle of a document, you'll know what I mean!

In fact, you've been using templates and styles all along, although you may not know it yet. Unless you've selected a different template, you're probably using the Normal document template, which is based on Word's factory settings. The Normal template comes with built-in styles; just click on the arrow button beside the drop-down list to ʾe them.

Not surprisingly, there are all sorts of slick tricks you can do with templates and styles.

Seeing What Kind of Formatting Has Been Applied

All you need to do to see what formatting is being applied to text is click the **Help** button on the **Standard** toolbar and then point to and click on the text whose formatting you want to check. You'll see a box showing what paragraph and character styles have been applied. You may recall this trick from Chapter 3.

Word's Factory Settings   The Normal document template uses 10-point Times Roman as the text font, with no automatic paragraph indents or extra line space before or after them, and tab stops are set every half inch.

Styles for three levels of headings—1, 2, and 3—come with the Normal template. Heading 1 is 14-point Arial (Helv is used if you don't have TrueType fonts), bold. Heading 2 is 12-point Arial bold italics, and heading 3 is 12-point Times Roman bold.

The Normal template also assumes you're using the U.S. English language dictionary.

Review Changes When AutoFormatting

If you want to be able to review changes, use the AutoFormat command on the Format menu instead of a shortcut. Word automatically formats your document if you press **Ctrl+K** or click the **AutoFormat** button (you can press **Esc** to cancel the process). If you want to be able to review and control the changes it makes, choose **AutoFormat** from the **Format** menu (**Alt, o, a**). After Word finishes formatting your document, you can go back and review each change it made (see Figure 8.3).

Keep the **Find Next after Reject** box checked to speed up your review. That way, Word moves quickly to the next formatting change each time you reject a change.

Applying Styles Automatically with AutoFormat

Word has an AutoFormat feature that will automatically go through a document and apply styles. To use it, click the **AutoFormat** button on the **Standard** toolbar or use the shortcut **Ctrl+K**. It's truly an amazing feature. Just keep a few things in mind as you create a document so that Word will be able to figure out what's what:

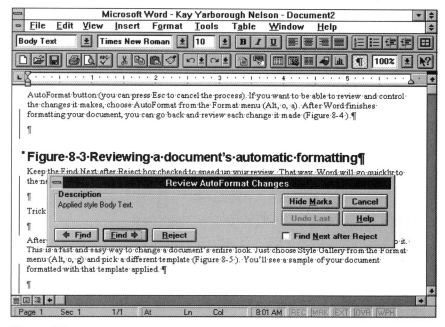

Figure 8.3 **Reviewing a document's automatic formatting**

♦ Press **Enter** to insert an extra paragraph mark above text that you want Word to format as a heading.

♦ Type a hyphen at the beginning of each line that you want formatted as a bulleted list.

♦ Type numbers followed by periods at the beginning of each line you want formatted as a numbered list (Word automatically corrects your numbering for you).

AutoFormat also automatically strips out extra blank lines between paragraphs, replaces straight quotes with curly quotes, and removes tab indents you've used to begin paragraphs with.

Use the Style Gallery Along with AutoFormat

After you've had Word automatically format a document, you may want to apply a different template to it. This is a fast and easy way to change a document's entire look. Just click on the **Style Gallery** button in the **AutoFormat** dialog box that appears when Word has finished autoformatting a document. Pick a different template (see Figure 8.4), and

Word for Windows 6.0 Slick Tricks

Figure 8.4 Click Style Gallery to view different styles.

you'll see a sample of your document formatted with that template applied.

Use Word's Wizards!

Word comes with specialized templates called Wizards. Try one out before you go any further—they're amazing, and using them can really save you a lot of time. The trick to using Wizards is that you have to choose **New** from the **File** menu. You'll see a list (see Figure 8.5) of the Wizards and templates you can use.

You'll be prompted throughout the process of creating the whole document. Afterward, you can change the document any way you like.

Open the Style Dialog Box Quickly

This is a handy shortcut to remember: Pressing **Ctrl+Shift+S** twice takes you directly to the Style dialog box (Figure 8.6). It's faster than reaching for the mouse.

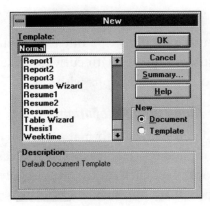

Figure 8.5 Selecting a Wizard

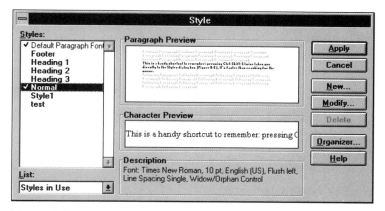

Figure 8.6 The Style dialog box

Changing the Default Template

All the documents you create when you click the New Document icon will be based on the Normal template. If you don't like certain things about the Normal template, it's easy to change it. For example, you can change the Normal template to add space between paragraphs. First, click on the **New Document** icon. Press **Ctrl+Shift+S** twice to open the **Style** dialog box. Choose **Normal** and click on **Modify**. You'll see the dialog box shown in Figure 8.7. Then click on the **Format** drop-down button, and pick **Paragraph**.

Now all you need to do is change the Spacing Before to whatever you'd like, and change any of the other settings while you're at it. The

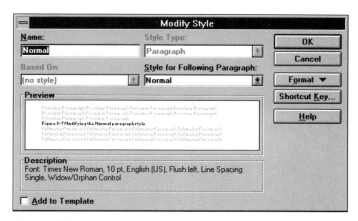

Figure 8.7 Modifying the Normal paragraph style

Preview box shows the effect of your settings. Then click OK to go back through the dialog boxes. Finally, click on **Apply** to get back to your document

That's it. Now your paragraphs will have an extra line of space between them. When you exit from Word, you'll be asked whether you want to save the global glossary and style changes; say **Yes**.

Changing the Margins

To change the page margins, you don't change the Normal template in any of the Styles dialog boxes that you saw in the preceding trick. Instead, double-click on the ruler to open the Page Setup dialog box and do it there. Click the **Default** button and say **Yes** when Word asks you if you want to change the Normal template.

Creating a New Template

Although you can create a template from scratch, the slickest, easiest thing to do is set up a document the way you want it and then convert it to a template you can use again and again. Remember: You can create a template from a document that has itself been created from a template or by a Wizard, after you've customized the document to suit yourself. Here's the general way to do it:

1. Once you've created the document, save it as a document (the normal way) so that you can use it by itself. The next thing to do is delete anything that you don't want to be part of the template, such as the text of a letter or memo. You can leave boilerplate text—text that you'll use in all the documents created with this template, or you can leave some placeholder text to remind you of what you're supposed to type.

2. After you've removed anything in the document that you don't want to appear in the template, replace the standard elements—such as the date, time, or author's name—with fields, as you saw earlier in this chapter.

3. If there's a date in your document, select it and choose **Insert Date and Time** from the **Insert** menu (**Alt, i, t**). Pick

the format you want to use and click OK. The date will appear in the document; press **Shift+F9** to display the actual field code. Be sure to leave the paragraph mark after the date field if you want it on a line by itself.

4 If there are elements in the document that will require you to do some typing, set them up so that Word will prompt you for what to type. This is a slick trick, and it's easy. At the point where you'll need to type, select any text that is there—such as the To: or Subject: part of a memo—and replace it with a different kind of field. Press **Ctrl+F9** to insert a field; then type fillin. Press the spacebar and type the message you want to display, enclosed in double quotation marks. For example, if you're requesting the user to enter the subject of a memo, type something like "Enter the memo's subject." Don't forget the quotes. Press the **Right arrow** key to move out of the field.

5 Look again at the document to see if there are any other places that could be automated with fields. For example, you might want to insert your name automatically by putting in an Author field (Word uses whatever is in the Summary Information box's Author box; press **Alt, f, i** to see what this is.) Or you might want to insert your return address with a UserAddress field, in which case Word uses the return address you use for envelopes.

6 Finally, you're ready to save the document as a template. Choose **Save As** from the **File** menu (**Alt, f, a**). Give your template a name, and under **Save File as Type**, choose **Document Template**.

To use your new template, choose **New** from the **File** menu (**Alt, f, n**) and select it. When the template opens, select the entire document by pressing Ctrl+A and then press **F9** to update all the fields. You'll get dialog boxes for all the fill-in fields you inserted; fill them out, and your boilerplate document is created.

Changing the Normal Template

If you want to change the formatting that the Normal template uses, here's how: Press **Ctrl+O** and, under **List Files of Type**, choose **Template**. Navigate to the directory where Word keeps the templates. Usually, this is c:\winword. Then select **normal.dot**. Go ahead and make any changes you want, such as changing the font and point size, line spacing, or anything else you'd like. Now, save the document. The next time you create a new document, Word will use these new settings.

Display All the Styles That Come with Word

You get over 30 different preset styles with Word, but you normally see only a few of them (only the ones that have been applied in your document) when you click on the Style button in the Standard toolbar. To view all the styles, click on the **Styles** button with the **Shift** key held down (see Figure 8.8).

Reapplying a Style

When would you want to reapply a style? Say that you've done some "local" formatting—applying additional formatting to paragraphs, such

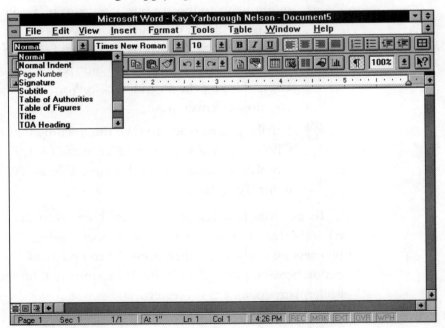

Figure 8.8   Some of the styles that come with Word

as flush right or centering. Then you decide you want to go back to the paragraph's original style. Don't bother removing the formatting you've applied; just select the paragraph (or several paragraphs) that you want to revert to the original style and press **Ctrl+Q**.

Use Keyboard Shortcuts When Defining Styles

This is a *really* neat trick. You may not be aware of it, but you can also use most of the same keyboard shortcuts you use for formatting in a document to define formatting in a style. When modifying a style or creating a new one, just type the keyboard shortcut for the formatting you want to use. For example, use **Ctrl+E** for Center, **Ctrl+T** for a hanging indent, **Ctrl+I** for italics, **Ctrl+B** for bold, **Ctrl+2** for double spacing, and so on. Review Chapter 3 for more formatting keyboard shortcuts.

Got a Favorite Style? Give It a Keyboard Shortcut.

If there's a style you use a lot, assign a keyboard shortcut to it. Select **Style** from the **Tools** menu to open the **Style** dialog box, click on the **Modify** button, and then click the Shortcut Key button. Then, in the Customize dialog box that appears (see Figure 8.9) press the keys that you want to assign to that style.

Don't do this for styles you rarely use, because you'll never remember all those shortcuts. Save the easy-to-remember shortcuts for styles you

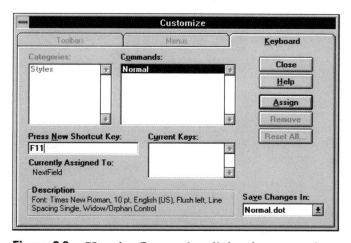

Figure 8.9   Use the Customize dialog box to assign a shortcut key to a style

use every day. If a shortcut has already been assigned to another feature, you'll see what it's been assigned to if you try to use that combination.

You can use the letters A through N (uppercase and lowercase are the same), the numbers 0–9, the function keys F2 through F12 (F1 is reserved for Help), and Ins and Del. Be careful about assigning key combinations that are already in use. Word has already taken the best of them (the mnemonic ones that are easiest to remember) for itself.

Saving Style Changes in a Template Isn't Automatic

If you're setting up styles in a template, you need to take an additional step to make sure that they get saved with the template. To start defining styles, press **Shift+Ctrl+S** twice and click on **New** or **Modify**, depending on whether you're creating a new style from scratch, or modifying an existing one. Then, in the **New Style** (see Figure 8.10) or **Modify Style** dialog box, check the **Add to Template** box. Finally, go ahead and create or edit the style.

Displaying Style Names

Word has a Style area to the left of the document that displays the name of the style each paragraph is using. Normally this area isn't visible, but you can display it; this can be useful in a document that switches back and forth between several styles. Choose **Options** from the **Tools** menu

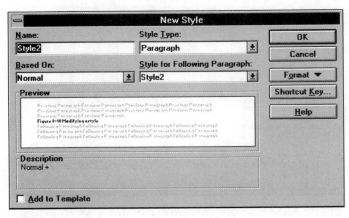

Figure 8.10 Creating a new style

and click the **View** tab. In the **Style Area Width** box, set a width that can display the longest style name. Make a guess; you can easily adjust it later. When you click OK to return to the document, you'll see style names on the left of the screen. Just drag the dividing line to make it wider or narrower.

Create a Style from an Existing Paragraph

After you've got a paragraph formatted the way you like it, make that formatting into a style. With the insertion point anywhere in the paragraph, press **Shift+Ctrl+S** twice to bring up the **Style** dialog box, and click on **New**. Type a new name for the style. Be sure to use a name that is different from any existing style name. Click OK and Close to return to your document. You'll see the new style in the style list when you display it.

Applying the Next Higher or Lower Heading Style

Now, this is a slick trick. If you're using several different heading levels in a document—say, heading 1 through heading 4—just put the cursor anywhere in the heading and press **Alt+Shift+Left arrow** to make that heading one level higher or **Alt+Shift+Right arrow** to make it one level lower. You can have as many as nine different heading levels in a document.

Shortcuts for Applying Other Styles

Use **Ctrl+Shift+L** to apply the bulleted list style. Use **Ctrl+Shift+N** to apply Normal style.

Changing Headings in Outline View by Dragging

To change a heading to the next higher or next lower style in Outline view, just drag it. Drag toward the left margin to increase the level, or toward the right margin to make it a lower-level heading.

Changing Headings in Outline View with Icons

Look at Figure 8.11; you can just click on those icons to change a heading into a higher or lower level, or change a heading into body text.

Use Outline Numbering for Headings in a Document

If you use the Outline method of numbering headings in a document, you get two benefits: First, headings will always be numbered accurately,

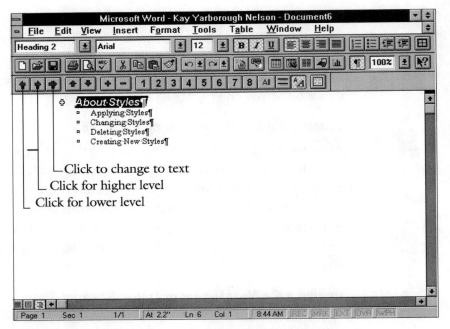

Figure 8.11 Click to change heading levels in Outline view

even if you cut and paste large sections of your document. Second, you can collapse an outline to see its structure quickly and decide which section to go to next, without reading screens full of text.

Copying a Paragraph's Style with the Format Painter

This has already been mentioned (in Chapter 3), but here it is again—because this is such a slick trick. To apply one paragraph's formatting to another, select the paragraph that has already been formatted the way you want. Then click on the **Format Painter** icon on the **Standard** toolbar, and select the paragraph that you want to reformat. The style of the first paragraph is applied to the second, without your having to choose a style name from a list, or even know what the style's name is, for that matter!

Another way to do the same thing, using the keyboard instead of the mouse, is to apply a style to one paragraph; then select the next paragraph you want to apply that same style to and press **Ctrl+Y**.

Use the "Style for Following Paragraph" Feature

Choose **Style** from the **Format** menu and select **New** or **Modify** to create a new style. Using Word's Style for Following Paragraph feature lets you switch to a different style as soon as you press the Enter key. It's a great way to set up styles for headings and lists in documents, because as soon as you type the heading and press Enter, you switch back to the body text style without having to pick it.

While you're in the **New Style** or **Modify Style** dialog box, pick the style you want to use for the next paragraph from the list under **Style for Following Paragraph**. Usually, you'll switch back to Normal style.

Print Out Your Styles

Word comes with many built-in styles, and you'll probably add new ones to them. It can get hard to remember what's what after you've created a few styles. To get a printout of your styles and their individual specifications, choose **Print** from the **File** menu (**Alt, f, p**) and then choose **Styles** from the **Print What** list.

Slick Macro Tricks

Relax! We're not going to cover Word's complex macro language (WordBasic) here. But Word comes with lots of macros that have already been created, and they can make your work much simpler. In this section, you'll see some slick macro tricks, and they're easy.

The easiest way to use Word's macros feature is to use the ones that come with the program. In fact, you may not even be aware that all sorts of prerecorded macros are available to you. But you can also record a few easy macros on your own—without using any programming language.

Recording a Macro

It's easy to record a macro, because Word simply remembers everything you do. If you make a mistake, correct it, and the steps used to correct the mistake are also recorded. Here's the quick way to do it:

1 Double-click on the **REC** indicator on the status bar.

2 Type a name for the macro and enter a short (optional) description of what it does in the **Record Macro** dialog box (see Figure 8.12).

3 Click OK. You'll see the Macro Record toolbar, and the mouse pointer changes into a pointer with a cassette attached to it (see Figure 8.13). You'll also see "REC" on the status bar to indicate that everything you do will be recorded.

4 Type whatever you want to record. Use formatting commands, menu commands, dialog boxes—do whatever you'd normally do (but see the next Trap). If you make a mistake, click on the **Undo** button on the **Standard** toolbar, or just correct the mistake.

5 To stop the macro recorder when you're done, click on the **Stop** button on the **Record Macro** toolbar, or double-click on the **REC** indicator on the status bar.

That's it—you've recorded a macro! Here are some ideas for other macros you might want to record:

♦ A macro that creates your letterhead and centers it on the page.

♦ A macro that types a phrase you use over and over again, such as "to meet the schedule as defined in the document named Jones proposal dated February 16, 1994."

Figure 8.12 Recording a macro

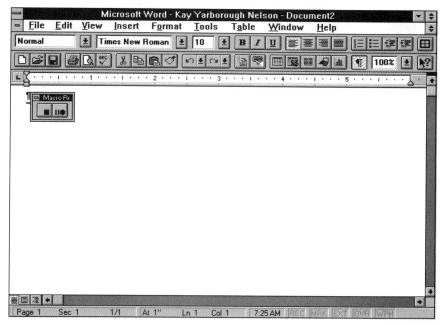

Figure 8.13 The Record Macro toolbar appears when you're recording a macro.

- ♦ A macro that creates a special header or footer.
- ♦ A macro that transposes sentences or words (very useful if you do heavy editing).

The Macro Recorder Doesn't Record Certain Mouse Actions

Word faithfully records all the commands you give from the keyboard or from menus, but it has no way of recording where the insertion point is if you click with the mouse or select text with the mouse. Watch the pointer on the screen. If you can see that cassette that's attached to it, Word won't record what it does. If you click, you'll hear a beep. Use a keyboard equivalent (like the arrow keys) to move the insertion point. Press F8 and use the arrow keys to select text.

Assign a Macro to a Key Combination

If there's a macro you use often enough that you can remember another key shortcut for it, assign it to a key combination, because the most efficient way to use it is via the keyboard. Word makes assigning a macro to a key combination easy.

Before you click **OK** in the Record Macro dialog box, just click on the **Keyboard** button to get the **Customize** dialog box (see Figure 8.14). Type a key combination and click on **Assign**. Then click OK and record your macro.

You can assign a key combination when you're recording the macro, but you may not know at that time how valuable the macro will be. Here's how to go back and give it a shortcut.

1 Choose **Customize** from the **Tools** menu (**Alt, t, c**); then click on the **Keyboard** tab.

2 Select **Macros** from the **Categories** list.

3 Select the macro's name.

4 In the **Press New Shortcut Key** box, type the key combination you want to assign to the macro; then click on **Assign**.

Remember to say **Yes** to saving changes when you exit if you want to save the shortcut you just created so that you can use it again.

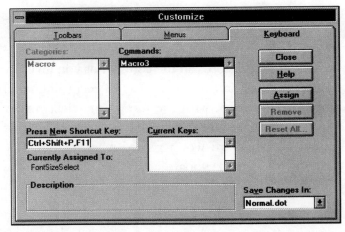

Figure 8.14 Assigning a key combination to a macro

Assign a Macro to a Key Combination for Just One Session

If you don't say Yes to macro changes when you exit, your macro will be "good" only for that one session with Word. This is a slick trick for using the same easy-to-remember key combo to insert different boiler-plate text in different Word sessions.

For example, on Wednesday **Ctrl+Shift+X** might type in a return address you're using over and over again, and on Thursday that same key combination can be used to type a completely different return address or a standard contract paragraph.

Remember One Simple Rule

Macros must be run under the same conditions they were recorded under in order to work. If you keep this one simple rule in mind, you'll eliminate many of the problems most people have with macros. For example, if you've selected a paragraph and record a macro that does something with that paragraph, Word expects you to always select a paragraph *before* you run the macro.

You can use a description of as many as 99 characters for a macro, so if it needs a special condition to run under, put that in the Description box when you record the macro so that you won't forget it.

Look at the List of the Macros That Come with Word

Before you spend any time recording macros, check out the prepackaged macros that come with Word. Word comes with lots of built-in macros. To see them, choose **Macro** from the **Tools** menu (**Alt, t, m**) (see Figure 8.15).

Specialized macros are also included with Word's templates. To see them, choose **Macro** from the **Tools** menu and click on the **Organizer** button in the **Macro** dialog box. Click on the **Macros** tab (see Figure 8.16); then click on **Close File** to close NORMAL.DOT. Click on **Open File** and choose another template file, and check out the macros in it. You can copy them into Word's other templates.

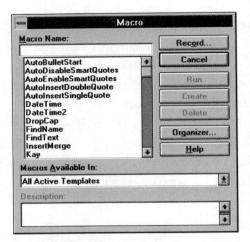

Figure 8.15 Word's prepackaged macros

Different Ways to Run a Macro

There are all sorts of different ways to run a macro. You can choose **Macro** from the **Tools** menu and select the macro you want, or you can assign the macro to a key combination, as you saw earlier.

You might also want to assign a favorite and often used macro to a menu or even to a toolbar button. You can even assign a macro to a field, but we won't go into that here.

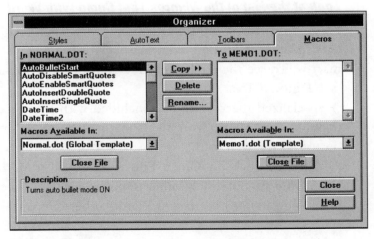

Figure 8.16 Copying macros in Word's templates

Assigning a Macro to a Button

If you want to be able to run a macro with a click of the mouse, make it into a button on the toolbar:

1 Display the toolbar you want to assign the macro to.

2 Choose **Customize** from the **Tools** menu and select the **Toolbars** tab.

3 Select the template that contains your macro from the **Save Changes In** list. Normally, this will be NORMAL.DOT and you don't have to worry about it.

4 From the **Categories** list, choose **Macros** and hoose the macro you want to add to the toolbar and drag it onto the toolbar.

5 Choose the button you want to use to represent that macro and click on **Assign**; then close the dialog boxes.

6 Choose **Save All** from the **File** menu to save your changes to that toolbar.

Assigning a Macro to a Menu

If you use a macro often, but not often enough to memorize a keyboard shortcut for it, put it on a menu.

1 Choose **Customize** from the **Tools** menu and click the **Menus** tab.

2 Select the template that contains your macro from the **Save Changes In** list. (Normally, this will be NORMAL.DOT.)

3 From the **Categories** list, choose **Macros**.

4 In the **Change What Menu** box, select the name of the menu you want the macro assigned to.

5 Use the **Position on Menu** box to indicate where you want the macro to appear on the menu.

6 Use the **Name on Menu** box to edit the macro's name as you want it to appear on the menu. Type an ampersand (**&**) before the letter you want to use as the shortcut key.

7 Click on **Add** and **Close**, and you'll see your macro on that menu when you open it.

Automatic Macros

You can create five macros that will run automatically under certain conditions:

- ◆ Any macro that you name AutoExec runs when you start Word.
- ◆ Any macro that you name AutoNew runs when you create a new document.
- ◆ Any macro that you name AutoOpen runs when you open a new document.
- ◆ Any macro that you name AutoClose runs when you close a document.
- ◆ Any macro that you name AutoExit runs when you exit Word.

For example, you might want to record a macro that opens the Save As dialog box and name it AutoNew. That way, you'll be reminded to give each new document a name before you even start typing. The AutoExec macro could be a macro that creates your letterhead or a special footer.

Prevent the AutoExec Macro from Running

Sometimes you may not want the AutoExec macro to run when you start Word. You can prevent the AutoExec macro from running on startup by holding the Shift key down as you start Word. Or you can start Word with a different macro; see the next trick.

Starting Word with a Macro

You've already seen this in Chapter 1, but here it is again in case you forgot:

- ◆ To start Word with a macro, give the command in the Program Manager's Run box as winword /mmacroname.
- ◆ To start Windows and Word from the DOS command prompt *and* start Word with a macro, use win winword /mmacroname.

Recording Macros Is Limited

The type of macro you can create by recording is limited. You can create much more sophisticated macros with WordBasic, Word's built-in macro language. If you record macros, you're limited by what you can actually do in the program. For example, if you want a macro to repeat an action over and over until it works on all occurrences of something in a document, you have to use the macro language, not the recorder.

Graphics Tricks

Word comes with a built-in drawing program. All you have to do to use it is click the Drawing button on the Standard toolbar, the one with the circle, square, and triangle on it. The Drawing toolbar appears, and you'll be in Page Layout view, ready to draw.

Drawing Rectangles and Squares

To make a rectangle, click on the **Rectangle** button. Click and drag while pressing **Ctrl** to draw a rectangle from the center outward (see Figure 8.17).

To draw a square, press **Shift** as you drag. To draw a square starting at its center, press **Ctrl+Shift** as you drag.

Drawing Lines at Various Angles

Press **Shift** as you draw a line so that the line will be drawn at a 30-, 60-, or 90-degree angle.

Drawing a Circle

To draw a perfect circle, press **Shift** as you drag. To draw a circle from the center outward, press **Ctrl+Shift**. To draw an oval (ellipse) from the center outward, press **Ctrl** as you drag.

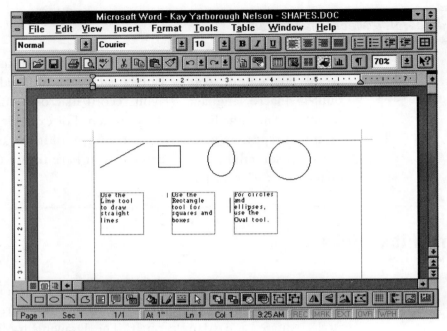

Figure 8.17   Drawing shapes

Drawing an Arc

The same tricks you just saw for drawing circles and rectangles apply to drawing arcs, too. To draw an arc that curves like a circle, press **Shift** as you drag. Press **Ctrl** to draw an arc from the center. Press **Ctrl+Shift** to draw a circular arc from its center.

Double-Click to Stop Drawing a Polygon

When you draw a shape with the Freeform tool, each line you draw is anchored when you click with the mouse. To stop drawing, double-click.

If a Graphic Image Isn't Available, Insert a Frame

Use the **Insert** menu and insert a frame as a placeholder if the graphic image you're trying to insert isn't available. It can act as a placeholder in the text so that your pagination stays accurate.

You Can Put Text in a Frame, Too

A frame can hold text as well as graphic images. You can create some very interesting effects this way, such as pull quotes. The advantage of

Drawing Programs vs. Painting Programs You may have used a painting program such as Windows Paintbrush before. A painting program isn't the same as a drawing program. In a painting program, you "paint" pixel by pixel (a pixel is the smallest screen element—think of it as a tiny dot on the screen). Your artwork is composed of tiny dots. You manipulate what you create in a painting program in a different way from the way you manipulate drawn objects in a drawing program. For example, if you add text in a painting program, it becomes a collection of pixels, just like any image that you've "painted," as soon as you click outside the text.

In a drawing program, the objects you create can be manipulated individually. You can, for example, select just one line that you've drawn and change it. To create a drawing, you draw the composite shapes and then put them together. Drawing programs are much more versatile than painting programs.

Pictures and drawings are different, too. In Word, a picture is a graphic image that you insert with the Insert Picture command. You can create a picture by using the Create Picture button on the Drawing toolbar (the one that looks like a mountain with a moon over it).

creating pull quotes in frames—as opposed to creating fancy borders around paragraphs, as you saw in Chapter 4—is that you can simply drag to reposition them on the page, or have the rest of the text on the page flow around them.

Here's how to create a pull quote like the one in Figure 8.18, shown in Print Preview.

1 Switch to Page Layout view so that you can see what's going on.

2 Select the paragraph that you want to make into a pull quote and choose **Frame** from the **Insert** menu (**Alt, i, f**). (If you haven't switched to Page Layout view, Word asks you if you want to switch.)

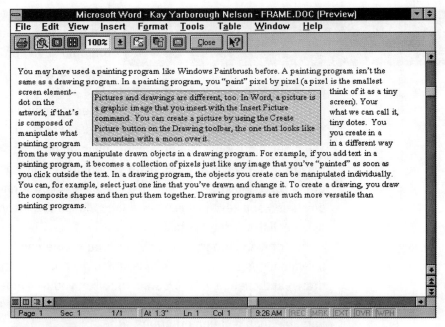

Figure 8.18 Creating a pull quote with text flowing around it

③ Drag the text frame to the location you want it on the page. You can resize it by dragging one of the handles on the frame inward or outward (if you don't see the handles, click on the side of the frame to select it.) Choose **Page Width** in the **Zoom** control box if you want to be able to see the entire page as you position the frame.

④ When you have the frame where you want it and it's the right size, click on the **Borders** button, and pick a border and shading for it to get the effect shown in Figure 8.18 (outside borders, 30% shading).

You can position the frame as you want it on the page (see Figure 8.19 for a variation). Select the frame, choose **Frame** from the **Format** menu, and use the **Frame** dialog box (see Figure 8.20) if you need to specify an exact horizontal or vertical position, set a size for the frame, anchor it to surrounding text, and so forth. If you want to specify that the frame be flush left or right on the page or column, instead of dragging it where you want it, you can choose **Left** or **Right** in the **Position** box under **Horizontal** as you create the frame.

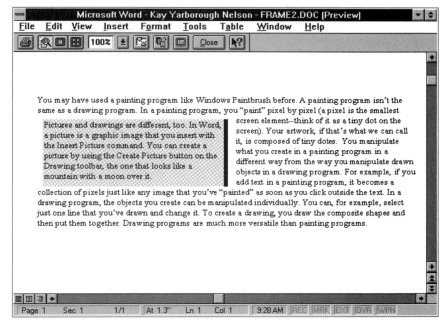

Figure 8.19 Creating a sidebar

Creating a Drop Cap

Using a drop cap—a large initial capital letter at the beginning of a paragraph—is a sophisticated touch you might want to add to desktop-published documents. When you create a drop cap in Word, you're actually using a frame, although you may not be aware of it. Here's how to create a drop cap like the one shown in Figure 8.21.

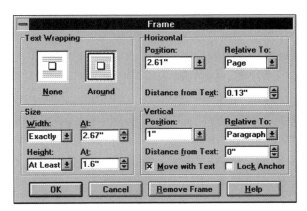

Figure 8.20 The Frame dialog box

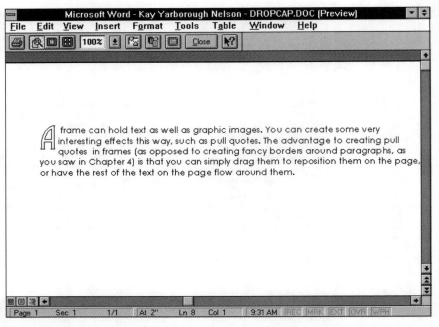

Figure 8.21 The finished drop cap in Page Layout view

1 Switch to Page Layout view so you can see what's happening. Drop caps don't display accurately in Normal view.

2 Select the letter you want to make into a drop cap. Normally, this is the letter beginning the first paragraph on the page.

3 Choose **Drop Cap** from the **Format** menu (**Alt, o, d**). You'll see the Drop Cap dialog box (see Figure 8.22).

4 Choose **Dropped** or **In Margin** and other options appear.

5 Choose the font you want to use and pick the number of lines to drop. You can also specify the space you want between the drop cap and the surrounding text.

6 Choose **OK** and Word puts a frame around the selected letter and changes it to the font, position, and size you chose, as shown in Figure 8.21.

Since the drop cap is in a frame, you can select it and drag it to a different position on the page.

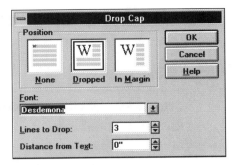

Figure 8.22 The Drop Cap dialog box

Using a Graphic As a Watermark

A watermark is text or a graphic image that appears to be printed "behind" the text on every page of a document. The trick to creating a watermark is to put it in a header or footer and then put that header or footer where you want the watermark to appear on the page. Here's how to create one right in the middle of a page (instead of at the top or bottom, where headers and footers normally appear).

1 Click on the **Drawing** button on the **Standard** toolbar, and choose **Header and Footer** from the **View** menu.

2 Click on the **Show/Hide Document Text** button on the **Header and Footer** toolbar. Click in the middle of the vertical scroll bar to go to the middle of the page.

3 Click on the **Text Box** button on the **Drawing** toolbar. Draw a text box the same size as the graphic image you want to use as a watermark.

4 Choose **Format Drawing Object** from the **Format** menu (**Alt, o, o**), click on the **Line** tab, and click on **None** and **OK**, because you probably don't want a border (which Word normally puts around text boxes) around a watermark.

5 Choose **Picture** from the **Insert** menu and double-click on the graphic image you want to use. In our example, it's **books.wmf**.

6 Click on the **Fill Color** and **Line Color** buttons, and select a gray. With the drawing object selected (so that you can see handles around it, as shown in Figure 8.23), click on the **Send Behind Text** button on the **Drawing** toolbar.

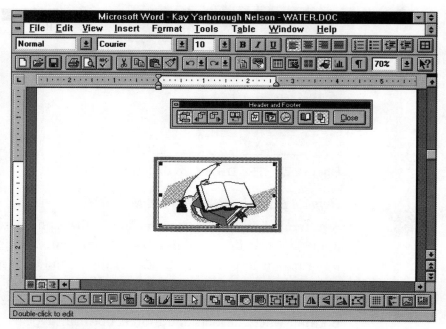

Figure 8.23 Creating a watermark

7 Switch to Print Preview to view your watermark. It won't display in Normal view.

8 Type the text of your document, or cut and paste it from another file. As a last check, you can go back to Print Preview again to view the results (see Figure 8.24).

If your watermark looks too dark when you print it, change the fill colors to a lighter gray.

Using Text As a Watermark

If you want to use text (such as "confidential") as a watermark, try this slick trick: Start setting up a header or footer, as in the preceding trick. Use the **Text Box** button on the **Drawing** toolbar to create a text box. Instead of inserting a picture, type the text you want to appear on the pages of your document in the text box, and then click on the **Send Behind Text** button to place that text behind the regular text.

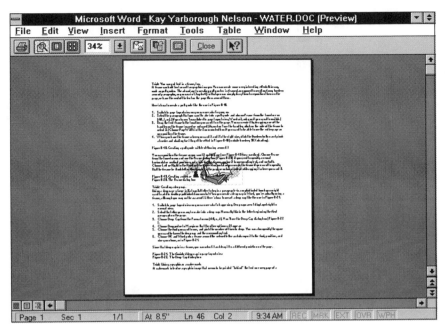

Figure 8.24   Viewing a watermark in Print Preview

What Next?

. . . .

We've reached the end of this compendium of tricks for Word for Windows, but we've by no means covered everything. Exploring the program's extensive Help system on your own is an excellent way to start down the path of mastering the more technical and sophisticated aspects of Word for Windows.

Index

A

advanced searches, 24
aligning text, 80
  in headers and footers, 104
all caps, 33
alphabetizing in tables, 173–175
Alt key menu shortcuts, 1–2
Alt+backspace (undo), 34
Alt+Ctrl+A (annotate), 52
Alt+F4 (save and exit), 19
Alt+Hyphen (document Control menu), 9
Alt+Shift+P (insert page number) 108
Alt+Spacebar (Word Control menu), 9
Alt+Tab (switch program), 8
annotating a document, 52–53, 54–55

annotations, printing, 181
applying styles, 76
  with AutoFormat, 202–203
arcs, drawing, 221
Arrange All command, 7
ascenders, 64
AutoCorrect, 43–48
  for dashes, 90
  and special symbols, 91–92
AutoExec macro, 220
AUTOEXEC.BAT, editing to start Word and Windows, 28
AutoFormat, 202
  options, changing, 148
  and special characters, 92
automatic macros, 220
automatic saving, 144
automatic typing. *See* AutoCorrect
automatic word selection, 138
AutoText, 43–48
  and tables, 171–172

Ctrl+F6 (next document), 9
Ctrl+G (Go To), 50–51
Ctrl+H (replace), 57
Ctrl+Home (top of document), 36
Ctrl+Ins (copy), 40
Ctrl+J (justify), 80, 81
Ctrl+L (left align), 80, 81
Ctrl+M (indent), 71
Ctrl+N (new document), 22
Ctrl+O (open), 16
Ctrl+Q (remove paragraph formatting), 71
Ctrl+R (right align), 80, 81
Ctrl+S (save), 16
Ctrl+Shift+F5 (bookmark), 51
Ctrl+spacebar (clear character formatting), 61, 86
Ctrl+T (hanging indent), 70
Ctrl+Tab, in dialog boxes, 12
Ctrl+V (paste), 42
Ctrl+W (close window), 9
Ctrl+Y (repeat typing), 32
Ctrl+Z (undo), 34
Ctrl-clicking, 37
curly quotes, 59, 90–92
custom dictionaries, 145–147
customizing Word, 123–148
Cut (Ctrl+X), 2
cutting in tables, 160–162
cutting text, 39–41

D

dashes, 90, 92
date
    displaying on startup, 198
    inserting the, 38, 197
    putting in headers and footers, 105–106
    setting the, 38–39

decimal tabs, 75
default directory, changing, 18, 141–143
default font, 123–124
default settings, 202
    starting with, 28
default template, changing the, 205–206
deleting files, 23–24
deleting in tables, 160
deleting words, 42–43
descenders, 64
deselecting, 38
dialog boxes, 12–14
dictionaries, changing, 145–147
displaying toolbars, 4
document
    opening a new, 22
    starting with a specific, 27
document statistics, 25–26
document summaries, 25
documents
    closing, 9, 21
    deleting, 23–24
    finding, 22, 24–25
    listed on File menu, 7
    listed on Window menu, 7
    moving between, 7–9
    moving through, 49–52
    opening several at once, 17
    read-only, 17
    saving all, 21
    viewing, 10
DOS, printing from, 181–183
dot leaders, using with tabs, 76
double indents, 81
double spacing, 77–78
dragging and dropping, 39–41
    in tables, 161–162
dragging to select, 37
drawing graphics shapes, 221–222
drives, switching, 19